Campgrounds of San Diego County

Federal, State, County, Regional, Municipal

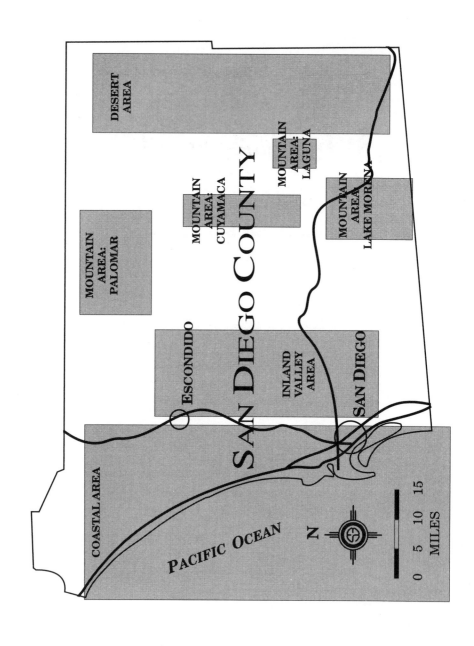

Campgrounds of San Diego County

Federal, State, County, Regional, Municipal

Jeff Tyler

Sunbelt Guidebooks and Maps
"Natural Adventures in the Californias"
A series edited by Lowell Lindsay

SUNBELT PUBLICATIONS
San Diego, California

Copyright © 2001 by Sunbelt Publications
All rights reserved. First edition 2001
Book design and composition by W. G. Hample & Associates
Project management by Jennifer Redmond
Cover design by Leah Cooper
Printed in the United States of America

Sunbelt Publications, Inc.
P.O. Box 191126
San Diego, CA 92159-1126
(619) 258-4911 (619) 258-4916 fax
www.sunbeltpub.com

05 04 03 02 01   5 4 3 2 1

Library of Congress Cataloging-in-Publication Data

Tyler, Jeff (Jeff H.)
    Campgrounds of San Diego County: federal, state, county,
    regional, municipal/Jeff Tyler.—1st. ed.
        p.cm.—(Sunbelt guidebooks and maps)
    Includes bibliographical references and index.
    ISBN 0-932653-43-X
        1. Camp sites, facilities, etc.—California—San Diego County—
    Guidebooks. 2. San Diego County (Calif.)—Guidebooks. I. Title.
    II Series

GV191.42.C2 T94 2000
647.9794 '9809'025—dc21

                                                00-053342

All photos by Jeff Tyler unless otherwise noted.
Cover photo: Digital imagery copyright 1998-2001 EyeWire, Inc.

Contents

vi

Preface

As a kid growing up in southern California, San Diego was the Coronado Islands, Navy ships, and the San Diego Zoo. Somewhere up in north county was the Palomar Observatory and over toward the east was a hair-raising road called Montezuma Grade which took you from mountain pines and junipers to palms and jojobas in seeming seconds. Later as an Angeleno doing occasional long weekends in tents, RVs, and camper shells, I found that there was more to San Diego than rocking and rolling off the Coronados and watching koalas in the zoo.

For example, the county has some of the best beachside public campgrounds on the coast. Inland, the observatory and Montezuma Grade are only parts of the county's many great camping areas. Best of all, these fine public campgrounds are maintained by taxpayer dollars, meaning their amenities can be enjoyed for minimal fees rather than paying an arm and leg.

Campgrounds are found beachside, lakeside, in pine forests at mile-high elevations, in city suburbs with easy access to supplies, in desert areas, and the list goes on. Facilities also vary, from full hookups and hot water showers (e. g., South Carlsbad State Beach), to unmarked, unpaved parking lot sites with a single, sometimes two, chemical toilets (e. g., Mountain Palm Springs). Several campgrounds resemble city parks, with well-kept expanses of lawn, well-pruned shade trees, toilet facilities and camping areas with paved camping spurs (e. g., Sweetwater Regional Park).

Most of the desert campgrounds lie within the largest contiguous state park (over 600,000 acres) in the United States, Anza-Borrego Desert State Park. Depending on seasonal rains, the wildflower displays in the spring at Anza-Borrego are spectacular. As might be expected, springtime reservations in Borrego's larger campgrounds are recommended as the camps fill quickly. The same applies to the California beach state park campgrounds during the summer months. All in all, for well-equipped public campgrounds in scenic areas, San Diego County public campgrounds are hard to beat.

Campgrounds of San Diego County, like others in this series for southern California, contains up-to-date, field-checked information on the county's public camps. Whether you're planning to camp in the comfort of your RV or in a tent pulled from the trunk of your car, I have endeavored to provide information you'll need

vii

for your next camping experience. For those of you who enjoy camping with your families, you'll find more information about day trips, activities and some private campgrounds in Judy Goldstein Botello's *More Adventures with Kids in San Diego*. While en route to your San Diego campsite, learn about our desert region from Diana Lindsay's *Anza-Borrego A to Z: People, Places, and Things*.

The book is divided into four major sections: Coastal Campgrounds, Inland Valley Campgrounds, Mountain Campgrounds and Desert Campgrounds. In addition, the Mountain Campground section is divided into four subsections, Palomar, Cuyamaca, Laguna, and Lake Morena. Within each area, campgrounds have been assigned numbers that correspond to their locations on our area map.

The descriptions contain information on the general settings and features of each campground: fees, restrictions, number of sites, contact information, and directions for getting there. In addition, the appendix includes a directory of useful phone numbers and addresses, as well as information on Adventure Passes, which are required for parking in the Cleveland National Forest.

Campground conditions can change rapidly—storm and fire damage, damage to access roads, budget constraints, and closings to protect sensitive habitats can all affect a campground. Campgrounds often fill up quickly during the summer months. When in doubt, phone the agency having jurisdiction over the campground before making the trip.

Note: Fees at California's state parks, which include state beaches and state recreation areas, were subject to change at the time of this writing, and may not agree with fees given in this book. Again, phone for details.

I wish to thank Rosalie and Leander Peik for their original vision and persistence in producing 21 editions of their earlier book, *Camper's Guide to San Diego County Campgrounds*, which inspired this book. I hope this book will meet the needs of today's campers as well. I've tried to provide accurate information, but if you find, after visiting a campground, that I've overlooked important features, I welcome your comments via correspondence to the publisher (see copyright page).

Jeff Tyler
January 2001
Rio Bravo, California

SAN DIEGO COUNTY
COASTAL AREA

▲ 1. San Onofre State Beach
    San Mateo Campground
    San Onofre Bluffs Campground
    Aliso Creek Rest Area
▲ 2. Guajome Regional Park
▲ 3. South Carlsbad State Beach
▲ 4. San Elijo State Beach
▲ 5. Silver Strand State Beach
▲ 6. Sweetwater Regional Park

1

San Onofre State Beach
San Mateo and San Onofre Bluffs Campgrounds

GENERAL SETTING (LOCATION, FEATURES, SUPPLIES, INFORMATION) This modest but attractive, 3000-acre state beach is somewhat remote and has a more natural appearance than other local beaches. Its two campgrounds lie close to the Orange County line, south of San Clemente. Visitors can enjoy swimming, surfing, and surf fishing in the Pacific Ocean, and sunning on the beach. *Caution:* Lifeguard service is provided only during summer.

San Mateo Campground, located about a mile inland from the ocean, sits on a low plateau overlooking a small valley to the south that is part of Camp Pendleton U.S. Marine Corps Base. Eucalyptus and pepper trees shade parts of the camp, and coastal shrubs afford some privacy. The mild marine climate makes camping pleasant most of the year; cool fog drifts over the ocean and coast on summer mornings. At times, a camp host resides in camp.

San Onofre Bluffs Campground consists of a series of parking spaces next to dirt sites, located along a 3-mile stretch of Basilone Road that traverses a bluff, about a mile south of San Onofre Nuclear Generating Plant. The road and bluff are parallel to the ocean and about a quarter mile from it. The elevation is 100 feet. Another rocky bluff separates the campground's bluff from the beach, and this bluff is easily visible from many parts of the campground. Some campsites have a view of the ocean in the distance, and other sites are separated by shrubbery that affords privacy. The campground is connected to the beach by several hiking trails. A few pepper trees and umbrella-shaped pines provide shade at the group site. A day-use picnic area is located near the entrance.

Supplies and gasoline are available near I-5 in San Clemente, about 5 miles north, and in Oceanside, about 17 miles south. For more information, write or phone San Onofre State Beach.

SITES, FEES, FACILITIES, TIME LIMITS San Mateo Camp has 157 numbered family campsites for tents or RVs, of which 67 have electrical and water hookups for $18 per site, nightly. The remaining 90 sites, without hookups, are available for $12 per site, nightly. Sites are dirt with some grass. Camp roads and parking spurs are blacktop. The maximum RV length is about 36 feet.

Each family campsite has a picnic table and a metal fire ring (with grill). Restrooms have sinks and flush toilets (some with wheelchair access). Some restrooms have hot (pay) showers. The camp has water spigots, outdoor laundry tubs, an RV water and dump station, trash cans, information boards, pay phones, and a newspaper vending machine near the entrance.

San Onofre Bluffs Campground has 176 numbered, mostly unshaded family campsites (no hookups). The fee is $12 per site, per night. Campsites are dirt. Camp roads and parking spaces are blacktop. The maximum RV length is about 30 feet.

Each family campsite has a picnic table and a metal fire ring (with grill). The camp has water spigots, an RV dump station, and trash cans. Pay phones are provided at two restrooms.

The group campsite, mainly for tent camping, accommodates 50 people and 12 vehicles. The group site's nightly fee is $50. The site is dirt and has a few picnic tables, concrete fire rings, benches, a water spigot, and trash cans. The blacktop parking lot has small parking spaces; the maximum RV length is about 18 feet.

San Onofre Bluffs day-use area has picnic tables, fire rings, benches, trash cans, and a blacktop parking lot. Two pay phones are located near the entrance. The day-use fee is $2 per vehicle.

Restrooms at San Onofre Bluffs' camping and day-use areas have pedal-flush toilets, outdoor sinks, and outdoor cold showers.

Reservations are recommended for family campsites and are required for the group campsite. No reservation fee is charged.

Dogs are allowed only on Trail 6. San Onofre State Beach's camps are usually open all year. The camping limit at family sites is 15 days, from June to September, and is 30 days, from October to May. The limit at the group site is seven days, year-round.

DIRECTIONS From central Oceanside, take I-5 north about 17 miles to Basilone Road. Exit and turn left (west), heading toward the ocean. Follow Basilone Road, as it turns south, and go 3 miles to San Onofre Bluffs Camp. Go north on I-5, beyond Basilone Road, about a mile to Cristianitos Road. Exit, turn right (east) and go a mile to San Mateo Camp on the right (south) side of the road.

Aliso Creek Rest Area

This CALTRANS rest area is a pleasant place to stop along the ocean between San Diego and San Clemente. The rest area resembles a park, with lawns and eucalyptus trees.

Some picnic tables are set on concrete slabs connected to the concrete pathways and are wheelchair-accessible. There are drinking fountains, vending machines (soft drinks and snack foods), benches, information boards, pay phones, newspaper vending machines, trash cans, recycling bins, and an RV dump station. Restrooms have sinks and some wheelchair-accessible flush toilets. The rest area is divided into two sections, one on each side of I-5, and is located about 6 miles north of Oceanside, where supplies and gasoline are available. The rest area is usually open.

Guajome Regional Park

GENERAL SETTING (LOCATION, FEATURES, SUPPLIES, INFORMATION) This stunning, suburban county park of more than 500 acres stretches over rolling knolls and is amply shaded by eucalyptus and pepper trees. It is located in eastern Oceanside near the Rancho Guajome Adobe home. At nearby Guajome Lake, free shore fishing is permitted. The park features two picnic areas with lawns and lake views, a playground, an enclosed pavilion, a gazebo, hiking trails, horseback riding trails, and a nature trail.

Rancho Guajome Adobe and the Antique Gas Steam Engine Museum are located about 2 miles south of the park. Weekend tours of the 28-room adobe house give history buffs and other visitors a taste of what life was like in early California. The museum presents displays of early-era farm equipment.

Mission San Luis Rey de Francia, 3 miles west of Guajome Park, is a quiet place for a stroll, and has a picnic area. Mission San Antonio de Pala, a mission asistencia with a small museum and gift shop, is located in Pala, about 16 miles northeast of Guajome Park, a short distance north of Highway 76. About 2 miles farther east is Wilderness Gardens Preserve, usually open, except during August; contact the San Diego County Parks' office for details. Hiking trails at the preserve are for day use only (the camp there is closed), and the parking fee is $2 per vehicle.

Supplies and gasoline are available on Highway 76 in eastern Oceanside and in the village of San Luis Rey, about 3 miles west. For more information (also regarding Wilderness Gardens), write or phone the San Diego County Parks' office.

SITES, FEES, FACILITIES, TIME LIMITS There are 34 numbered campsites with electrical and water hookups, of which 30 are for tents or RVs, and the remaining four are reserved for RVs only. The nightly fee is $14 per site. Reservations are required, for $3 per site. Sites are dirt with some grass. Camp roads and parking spurs are blacktop. The maximum RV length is about 45 feet.

Each campsite has a picnic table and a metal fire ring (with grill). The camp's restrooms have sinks, hot showers, and flush toilets (some with wheelchair access). The camp has water spigots, an RV dump station, trash cans, a dumpster, and an information board. A pay phone is located at the ranger station.

Picnic areas have picnic tables, pedestal barbecues, drinking fountains, restrooms, and blacktop parking lots. The day-use fee is $2 per vehicle. For each dog, the nightly fee or day-use fee is $1.

The campground at Guajome Regional Park is usually open all year. The camping limit is 14 days.

DIRECTIONS From I-5 in Oceanside, exit at Mission Avenue (State Highway 76). Go east about 7 miles to Guajome Lake Road, and turn right (south). Go a quarter mile to the park's main entrance, and turn right (west).

South Carlsbad State Beach

GENERAL SETTING (LOCATION, FEATURES, SUPPLIES, INFORMATION) Central Carlsbad with its many sights is north of this 100-acre state beach, and the village of Leucadia is not far south. Vast views of the Pacific Ocean are enjoyed from more than half the campsites, situated along a 3-mile bluff rising above the beach and ocean. The elevation is 50 feet. Several wooden stairways access the beach. Small, rounded myoprom trees separate campsites and provide privacy. There is little shade, but the pleasant coastal weather and ocean breezes make up for this. A South Pacific atmosphere is created by a few tall palms at the entrance.

Surfing, surf fishing, and swimming are popular at the ocean. *Caution:* Lifeguards are on duty only during summer. The campfire center is located near the entrance (see below). Interpretive programs are held occasionally during summer. At times, camp hosts reside at campsites 127 and 135.

Browse the art gallery and gift shop at the historic Alt Karlsbad Hanse House, with a taste of old German architecture. The small Carlsbad Children's Museum is specially designed for younger children. During spring, locally grown flowers bloom in colorful striped patterns in the large fields east of I-5.

Supplies and gasoline are available in Leucadia, about 3 miles south, and in Carlsbad, about 5 miles north. Limited supplies, ice, firewood, and beach rental equipment are available at the state beach's store (closed during winter). For more information, write or phone South Carlsbad State Beach.

SITES, FEES, FACILITIES, TIME LIMITS There are 222 numbered campsites for tents or RVs (no hookups). The nightly fee is

$12 per site. Reservations are strongly advised (no reservation fee); reserved sites are assigned by lottery at 9 A.M. each day. There are blacktop roads and dirt-and-gravel sites, but no parking spurs; parking is on the sites. The maximum RV length is about 35 feet.

Ten campsites are blacktop and are wheelchair accessible. Two of these sites have ocean views.

Each campsite has a picnic table and a metal fire ring (with or without grill). Restrooms have sinks and flush toilets (some with wheelchair access). Some restrooms have hot (pay) showers. There are water spigots, drinking fountains (at restrooms), an RV dump station, trash cans, dumpsters, and recycling bins. A (pay) laundry room, a newspaper vending machine, and a pay phone are available at the beach store. Another pay phone is located at the state beach office. The campfire center has a concrete fire ring, benches, and a few picnic tables.

Dogs are not allowed on the beach next to camp. The camp is usually open all year. The camping limit is seven days, from June to September, and is 15 days, from October to May.

DIRECTIONS From Encinitas, take I-5 north about 5 miles and exit at Palomar Airport Road (County Highway S-12) in Carlsbad. Turn left (west), and go about half a mile. Follow the sign that says CARLSBAD BOULEVARD SOUTH, and bear to the right on the off-ramp which curves around to Carlsbad Boulevard (County Highway S-21) going southbound. Go 1.5 miles to the state beach entrance. Turn right (west), and go to the entrance station.

San Elijo State Beach

GENERAL SETTING (LOCATION, FEATURES, SUPPLIES, INFORMATION) Striking sunsets enhance the sweeping view of the ocean from this 39-acre state beach at scenic Cardiff-by-the-Sea. Campsites sit on a low-lying bluff above the shore, at an elevation of 50 feet. Sites are separated by coastal shrubs that give privacy. Palm trees scattered throughout the campground lend a tropical touch. Some sites have views of the beach and the ocean below. Wooden stairways connect the campground to the beach. Cacti, yuccas, and other plants grow in a small garden at the state beach's office, and signs identify the plants. Sunning, surfing, surf fishing and swimming are some of the activities to take part in. *Caution:* Lifeguards are on duty only during summer. The day-use area is located north of camp. The campground features a campfire center. At times, camp hosts reside at sites 55 and 161.

Quail Botanical Gardens, located in Encinitas, about 2.5 miles north of camp, features native plants and rare, non-native plants. The gardens are open daily, with tours on Saturdays, and the parking fee is $2 per vehicle (no pets allowed). Downtown Del Mar, about 5 miles south of camp, resembles a traditional English village. The Del Mar Fair takes place during early summer and is held at the Del Mar Fairgrounds, just north of town. La Jolla, a few miles south of Del Mar, is known for its upscale shops, restaurants, and hillside homes with ocean views. Mount Soledad (Soledad Mountain) commands a view of La Jolla and the ocean.

Supplies and gasoline are available in Cardiff-by-the-Sea, in Encinitas, a few miles north, and in Solana Beach, a few miles south. Limited supplies, ice, and beach rental equipment are available at the state beach's store (close during winter). For more information, write or phone San Elijo State Beach.

SITES, FEES, FACILITIES, TIME LIMITS There are 30 sites with full hookups for RVs or tents, for $18 per site, per night, and 141 sites without hookups for RVs or tents, for $12 per site, per night. Reservations are advised (no reservation fee); reserved sites are assigned by lottery at 9 A.M. each day. Roads are blacktop; sites are dirt and gravel. Some sites have blacktop parking spurs. Where there are no spurs, parking is on the sites. The maximum RV length is about 35 feet. Five non-hookup wheelchair sites are blacktop.

Each site is numbered and has a picnic table and a metal fire ring (with grill). Restrooms have sinks, flush toilets (some with wheelchair access), and hot (pay) showers. The camp has water spigots, drinking fountains (at restrooms), outdoor cold showers, an RV dump station, trash cans, dumpsters, and recycling bins.

A (pay) laundry room, a newspaper vending machine, and a few picnic tables with ocean views are located at the beach store. Pay phones are provided at the store and at the office.

The day-use area has two picnic tables, a restroom, trash cans, a blacktop parking lot, and its own entrance, north of camp. The day-use parking fee is $2 per vehicle.

Dogs are not allowed on the beach next to camp. The camp is usually open all year. The camping limit is seven days, from June to September, and is 15 days, from October to May.

DIRECTIONS From I-5 in Encinitas, take Encinitas Boulevard west about half a mile to First Street (County Highway S-21). Turn left (south) and go about 2 miles. Pass by the day-use area, then arrive at the camping area entrance and turn right (west).

Silver Strand State Beach

GENERAL SETTING (LOCATION, FEATURES, SUPPLIES, INFORMATION) This state beach of more than 400 acres is located between Imperial Beach and downtown Coronado. It is situated on the Pacific Ocean side of the Silver Strand, a narrow strip of land that separates San Diego Bay from the ocean and connects Coronado to Imperial Beach. Seashells give the sandy shore a silvery appearance, hence the name. The camping area is a large, sea-level, blacktop parking lot by the beach, and the campsites are parking spaces in this lot. Some sites are next to the beach and have ocean views. The state beach has a large day-use area.

The historic Hotel del Coronado is located about 4.5 miles north of the state beach. This huge, charming, Victorian-era hotel is Coronado's most famous attraction and is the centerpiece of the city's downtown area. The San Diego-Coronado Bay Bridge, linking Coronado to central San Diego, is more than 2 miles long, and is San Diego County's longest bridge.

This state beach has the closest public campground to downtown San Diego, about 10 miles northeast via the bridge over the bay. Balboa Park, a municipal woodland of more than two square miles, boasts gardens, the world-renowned San Diego Zoo, Reuben H. Fleet Space Theater and Science Center, and several highly-regarded museums, including the San Diego Museum of Art, the Museum of San Diego History, the San Diego Museum of Man (culture), and the San Diego Natural History Museum (wildlife and plant life).

Old Town San Diego State Historic Park, near the junction of I-5 and I-8, includes the old plaza area where downtown San Diego was originally located, and features several examples of early California's Mexican architecture. For families with children, Sea World marine park on Mission Bay offers aquariums, rides, and a sky tower and aerial tram that afford wide views of Mission Bay and the surrounding area. Belmont Park features shops, a roller coaster and carousel, and is located at Mission Beach, a strand that separates Mission Bay from the ocean.

Surf fishing and swimming are available close to camp. *Caution:* Lifeguard service is limited. A blacktop bicycle path runs along the Silver Strand's eastern coast, next to San Diego Bay.

At times, a campground host is present in camp. A snack bar, beach rental equipment, ice, and charcoal are available during summer next to the ranger's office in the day-use area. Supplies and gasoline are available on Highway 75 in Imperial Beach, about 3 miles south, and in Coronado, about 5 miles north. For more information, write or phone Silver Strand State Beach.

SITES, FEES, FACILITIES, TIME LIMITS There are 124 non-reservable, numbered, blacktop parking spaces suitable for RVs; no tents are allowed. The fee per site, for one night maximum, is $12. The maximum RV length is about 35 feet.

Concrete fire rings (without grills) are located several yards from each other on the beach, near the campsites. The camp's restrooms have dressing rooms, flush toilets (some with wheelchair access), outdoor sinks (wash basins), and outdoor cold showers. Piped water, a drinking fountain, a pay phone, a newspaper vending machine, and a trash can are available outside the restroom. Dumpsters are located in the parking lot.

The day-use area has restrooms, pay phones, and spacious blacktop parking lots. The day-use parking fee is $2 per vehicle.

Generators must be turned off between 8 P.M. and 10 A.M. Dogs are not allowed on the beach or on the bay shore on the east side of the Silver Strand. The Silver Strand State Beach campground is usually open all year. The camping limit is one night.

DIRECTIONS From I-8 in San Diego, take I-5 south about 14 miles. Exit at Palm Avenue (State Highway 75), south of Chula Vista. Go west about 2 miles, and in Imperial Beach, follow State Highway 75 as it bends to the right (north) and becomes Silver Strand Boulevard. Go about 3 miles farther, and turn left (west).

Sweetwater Regional Park

GENERAL SETTING (LOCATION, FEATURES, SUPPLIES, INFORMATION) This county park is located near Sweetwater Reservoir, east of the charming village of Bonita. *Bonita* means *pretty* in Spanish, and describes the village and surrounding countryside well. The park is 7 miles inland from San Diego Bay, and it benefits from the gentle coastal climate.

The park sits on a small, flat hill with views of Sunnyside to the south and of Sweetwater Reservoir to the east. San Miguel Mountain rises to an elevation of 2565 feet and dominates the skyline to the east. Some eucalyptus trees and transplanted short pines beautify the camp and provide a little shade; wooden fences add rustic charm.

A special feature is the equestrian camping section with its corrals. A gravel staging area, a picnic pavilion, a kitchen, and a loop trail for horseback riding are provided nearby. The equestrian camping section is separated from the non-equestrian section by an open, grassy, parklike area. Near the park entrance is another grassy, open area with a few trees and a small picnic area.

Supplies and gasoline are available in Bonita, a few miles west, and in Chula Vista, near I-5. For more information, write or phone the San Diego County Parks' office.

SITES, FEES, FACILITIES, TIME LIMITS All sites have electrical and water hookups for RVs. There are 15 reservable equestrian sites, of which 10 are back-in sites with two corrals each, and five are pull-through sites with one corral each. There are 33 reservable non-equestrian sites of which 16 are back-in sites, and 17 are pull-through sites. Two wheelchair-accessible, pull-through sites are paved. Six back-in sites and four pull-through sites are nonreservable. Nightly fees range from $14 to $16 per site. The reservation fee is $3 per site. Camp roads are blacktop; sites and spurs are dirt and gravel. The maximum RV length is about 36 feet at back-in sites, and about 45 feet at pull-through sites.

Each site is numbered and has a picnic table and a metal fire ring (with grill). The restroom has sinks, hot showers, and flush toilets (some with wheelchair access). The camp has water spigots, an RV water and dump station, dumpsters, and trash cans. A drinking fountain, a soft drink vending machine, a pay phone, and an information board are at the restroom. A concrete fire ring in a small grassy area near the restroom serves as a campfire center.

The picnic pavilion has picnic tables, some of which are on concrete slabs (wheelchair accessible), two large pedestal barbecues, trash cans, and a kitchen with a refrigerator, stoves, sinks, serving counters, and outdoor laundry tubs.

The picnic area near the entrance has picnic tables, pedestal barbecues, park benches, drinking fountains, trash cans, a blacktop parking lot, concrete pathways, and wheelchair-accessible picnic sites on concrete slabs.

A large picnic group requires a reservation (fee). The day-use fee is $2 per vehicle. The nightly fee or day-use fee is $1 per dog.

No swimming is allowed in the reservoir. The camp is usually open all year. The camping limit is 14 days.

DIRECTIONS From I-8 in San Diego, take I-805 south about 10 miles to Bonita Road (County Highway S-17) in Bonita. Exit and go east 3.5 miles. At the intersection where Bonita Road turns left (north), continue straight ahead (east) on San Miguel Road. Go a mile to Summit Meadow Road. Turn left (north) and go half a mile.

SAN DIEGO COUNTY INLAND VALLEY AREA

▲ 1. Dixon Lake Recreation Area
▲ 2. Dos Picos Regional Park
▲ 3. Mission Trails Regional Park
   Kumeyaay Campground
▲ 4. Santee Lakes Regional Park
▲ 5. Lake Jennings Regional Park

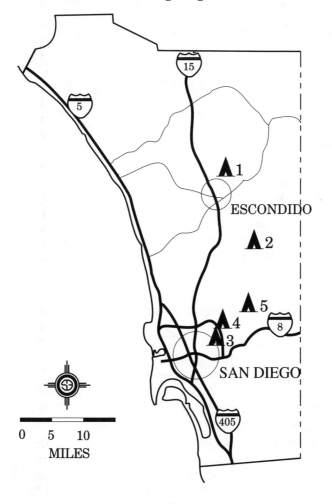

Dixon Lake Recreation Area

GENERAL SETTING (LOCATION, FEATURES, SUPPLIES, INFORMATION) The City of Escondido owns and operates this recreation area of more than 500 acres, including Dixon Lake, a domestic water source. Many campsites along a ridge have rustic views of the lake to the east and suburban views of Escondido to the west. The lake is surrounded by hills thickly covered with chaparral. Eucalyptus and other trees shade some sites, and bushes afford privacy. Campsites are spaced well apart.

The recreation area features a centrally located concession building by the lake, next to the ranger station. Hilltop Picnic Area and Jack Creek Picnic Area are located near the main entrance, and Lakeshore Picnic Area is near the concession building. These tree-shaded picnic areas have lawns, playgrounds, and views of the lake. An amphitheater (campfire center) is located in the campground. San Diego Wild Animal Park, a popular family attraction, is located on Highway 78, about 7.5 miles southeast of Dixon Lake Recreation Area.

The lake has a boat dock and three piers for fishing, one with wheelchair access. Fishing requires a daily permit and a fee. At the concession building, electric motors and boats for fishing are rented, bait is sold, and a room with fish-cleaning sinks is provided. Private boats and swimming are not allowed on the lake. Dirt-and-gravel parking lots are provided near fishing areas.

Supplies and gasoline are available in Escondido, a few miles west. A snack bar, a pay phone, and information boards are provided at Dixon Lake's concession building. For additional information, phone Dixon Lake Recreation Area.

SITES, FEES, FACILITIES, TIME LIMITS The camp has 45 numbered family campsites for tents or RVs. Ten of the sites have full hookups, for $16 per site, per night, and 35 sites have no hookups, for $12 per site, per night. The group camping loop, consisting of four adjacent family campsites, accommodates 50 people and 10 vehicles for $75 per night. The reservation fee is $5 per family site and $10 for the group loop. Some parking spurs are blacktop, and some are dirt and gravel; camp roads are blacktop. The maximum RV length is about 23 feet.

Each family campsite has a picnic table, a metal fire ring (with grill), and a wooden food locker. Four restrooms have sinks and flush toilets (some with wheelchair access). One restroom has hot showers. The campground has water spigots, drinking fountains (outside restrooms), an RV dump station, and trash cans.

The group camping loop has a 270-degree view, picnic tables, metal fire rings, and restrooms with sinks and flush toilets.

Picnic areas have picnic tables, pedestal barbecues, some shelters with service tables and electrical outlets, drinking fountains, restrooms, trash cans, and blacktop parking lots. Picnic reservations are accepted (fee). At the dirt-and-gravel parking lots, there are portable chemical toilets and trash cans.

The day-use parking fee, per vehicle, is $1 for vehicles up to 20 feet in length, and $3 for vehicles more than 20 feet in length. With a free Over-60 Card, senior citizens pay a reduced fishing fee and do not pay a day-use parking fee.

At Dixon Lake Recreation Area, no pets are allowed. Only charcoal may be used in the fire rings and barbecues. The campground is usually open throughout the year, and the camping limit is 14 days.

DIRECTIONS From I-15 in Escondido, exit at El Norte Parkway. Go east about 3 miles to La Honda Drive, turn north, and go about a mile to the entrance on the right (east) side of the road.

Dos Picos Regional Park

GENERAL SETTING (LOCATION, FEATURES, SUPPLIES, INFORMATION) Rugged, rocky peaks rise just west of this woodsy, semi-rural county park of nearly 80 acres, located southwest of Ramona. The park's name is well suited to the area, since *dos picos* means *two peaks* in Spanish. The park's camping and picnic areas and hiking trails have been pleasingly designed to fit in with the area's grand oaks and rolling terrain.

Adding to the rustic atmosphere is a wooden footbridge that crosses over an arroyo and leads through the woods to a duck pond. The park's nature trail connects this pond with the caravan camping area and includes an exercise course with signs.

The park features oak-shaded picnic areas, a playground, a soccer field, horseshoe pits, and a reception area.

For a side trip, visit Guy Woodward Museum, located inside a beautiful old home in nearby Ramona. Antiques paint a picture of the town's history.

Youth groups, such as scouts, may camp at two primitive county parks, Mount Gower Open Space Preserve, several miles east of

Ramona, and Hellhole Canyon Open Space Preserve (closed during August), several miles east of Valley Center. Each preserve has a primitive camping area and a staging area.

Supplies and gasoline are available in Ramona on Highway 67, about 5 miles east of the park, in Poway on Highway S-4, about 12 miles southwest, and in Escondido on Highway 78 near I-15, about 25 miles west. For more information, write or phone the San Diego County Parks' office.

SITES, FEES, FACILITIES, TIME LIMITS There are 50 numbered family RV sites with electrical and water hookups for $14 per site, per night, and 12 family tent sites without hookups for $10 per site, per night. The reservation fee for tent sites and 35 RV sites is $3 per site. The maximum RV length is about 40 feet.

Each family site has a picnic table and a metal fire ring (with grill) or a concrete barbecue, or both. The family camping area has water spigots, an RV dump station, and dumpsters. The family area's restroom has sinks, hot showers, and flush toilets.

The group caravan area accommodates 100 people and 22 RVs. The fee is $75 per night or $150 for the weekend, from 2 P.M. Friday to 2 P.M. Sunday. The caravan area is reservable (no reservation fee). It has picnic tables, a large fire ring, an enclosed pavilion, water, and a restroom (showers are located in the family area).

The youth group camping area is reached by a half-mile hike from the day-use parking lot. The fee is $35 per night, for up to three nights. This reservable area (no reservation fee) accommodates 25 youths with required adult supervision. It has picnic tables, a group fire ring, a water spigot, and portable toilets.

The park's picnic areas have picnic tables, pedestal barbecues, drinking fountains, dumpsters, restrooms nearby, and blacktop parking lots. The picnic area near the entrance holds up to 300 people, and a reservation (fee) is required for a large picnic group.

The day-use parking fee is $2 per vehicle. For each dog, the nightly fee or day-use fee is $1.

The park has a pay phone and an information board. A soft drink machine is outside the restroom near the entrance.

At Mount Gower and Hellhole Canyon Open Space Preserves, the nightly fee of $35 includes up to 48 youths who are 17 years of age or younger, with required adult supervision. Each preserve has portable toilets; no fires are allowed. Phone for more details.

Dos Picos' campground is usually open all year. The camping limit is 14 days. Quiet time is observed from 10 P.M. to 8 A.M.

DIRECTIONS From I-15 in Escondido, take State Highway 78 east about 20 miles. At State Highway 67 in Ramona, turn right (southwest). Go 3.5 miles, and at the fork, bear to the left and continue on Mussey Grade Road. Go a mile to Dos Picos Park Road, and turn right. Go 0.7 mile to the entrance.

Mission Trails Regional Park
Kumeyaay Campground

GENERAL SETTING (LOCATION, FEATURES, SUPPLIES, INFORMATION) The City of San Diego owns and operates this park of more than 5000 acres, located in the hills northeast of San Diego, between La Mesa and Santee. The park offers a sizable helping of hilly rural atmosphere in a location convenient to San Diego's urban area. Among the many features that lie within the park are Kumeyaay Campground, Kumeyaay Lake, Lake Murray, Mission Gorge, Cowles Mountain, Pyles Peak, Fortuna Mountain, Old Mission Dam, and 40 hiking trails.

Partly shaded Kumeyaay Campground sits on a gentle slope that drops a few yards below Father Serra Trail. Riparian trees separate the camp from the San Diego River. To the north, the Route 52 freeway bridge stands out against the hills. Hiking trails of less than 2 miles in length (one-way) open wide the surrounding area to exploration. Kumeyaay Lake Trail gives hikers views of nearby Kumeyaay Lake (formerly Hollins Lake). Oak Canyon Trail follows Oak Canyon north from Old Mission Dam historic landmark. Old Mission Dam is about half a mile west of camp, on Father Junipero Serra Trail. The dam was constructed in the early 1800s to enable irrigation of the land around Mission San Diego, several miles southwest. Grasslands Loop Trail is accessed from Father Junipero Serra Trail, west of camp. A day-use parking lot is provided at the eastern end of the campground.

Hiking is permitted along paved Father Junipero Serra Trail, which stretches south from camp about 2.5 miles to the park's headquarters, ranger station, visitor center, and gift shop, just north of Mission Gorge Road in San Carlos. *Note:* There are two intersections of Father Junipero Serra Trail and Mission Gorge Road—the southern one just mentioned, and the northern one, about a quarter mile east of camp, in Santee.

Lake Murray, on the northwestern edge of La Mesa, offers boating and fishing on weekends and Wednesdays, from November to Labor Day. The lake is stocked seasonally; fishing brings in bass, catfish, bluegill, and trout. Fishing requires a permit and a fee. Bait, tackle, and a snack bar are available at the concession building, and motorboats, rowboats, pedal boats, and canoes may be rented. The lake features a boat launch ramp (fee). The lake's picnic area has 10 barbecues, more than 50 picnic tables, and restrooms. Lake Murray Path is a popular trail with views of the lake.

La Mesa Depot Museum (trains) is located a few miles south of the park. Mission San Diego de Alcala, north of the junction of I-8 and I-15, features a museum and a distinctive bell tower.

At times, a camp host and a park ranger are present. Supplies and gasoline are available in Santee, in La Mesa near I-8, and in Tierrasanta near I-15 and Route 52. For information, contact Mission Trails Regional Park, or phone the ranger at Kumeyaay Camp.

Note: Finding nearby trails is fun and easy with Casey Cook's "Mission Trails Regional Park Trail Map," a Sunbelt publication.

SITES, FEES, FACILITIES, TIME LIMITS The campground has 46 numbered campsites (no hookups). Some sites are for RVs or tents; sites near Kumeyaay Lake are for tents only. The nightly fee is $12 per site. The camp's roads and parking spurs are paved; campsites are dirt. The maximum RV length is about 30 feet.

Each site has a picnic table. The camp has drinking water, trash cans, and restrooms with sinks, flush toilets, and hot showers.

No swimming is allowed. Dogs are not allowed within 50 feet of lakes and other water sources; the fee is $2 per dog.

Kumeyaay Campground is closed Tuesdays and Wednesdays, but is usually open otherwise. The camping limit is 14 days.

DIRECTIONS From I-8 in San Diego, take I-15 north 4.5 miles to State Route 52 (freeway) in Tierrasanta. Take Route 52 east about 7 miles to Mast Boulevard in Santee. Exit, turn left (east), and go a short way to West Hills Parkway. Turn right (south) and go about half a mile to Mission Gorge Road. Turn right (west) and go a quarter mile. At the OLD MISSION DAM sign, bear right (west); this road is Father Junipero Serra Trail. Go a quarter mile, and the camp is on road's right (north) side, opposite Bushy Hill Drive.

Santee Lakes Regional Park

GENERAL SETTING (LOCATION, FEATURES, SUPPLIES, INFORMATION) The Padre Dam Municipal Water District owns and operates this well-equipped park of nearly 200 acres, developed on the shores of seven reclaimed lakes. Water is filtered, flows through the lakes, and is then used for irrigation purposes. The park is located in Santee, roughly 20 miles east of San Diego.

Palms and oaks, ducks on the lakes, and the quiet hills nearby to the west provide a relaxing setting. The park has picnic areas and playgrounds. Some campsites and picnic sites have lake views. Trees shade some sites and picnic areas and provide privacy. For more about the local area, see Mission Trails Regional Park.

The campground's swimming pool is for registered campers. *Caution:* There are no lifeguards. A clubhouse in camp is available for group meetings. Volleyball courts and horseshoe pits are available in the day-use area; fees and deposits are required. Nature talks are periodically given; phone for information. The park has a general store where bait and tackle are available and rowboats, canoes, pedal boats, and sporting equipment can be rented. The lakes are stocked with trout, bass, and catfish. Fishing requires a permit and a fee. A fish-cleaning area is provided.

The park is patrolled. At times, camp hosts reside at campsites 35, 114, and 143. Supplies and gasoline are available nearby in Santee. At the park's general store, located between Lakes 4 and 5, propane and limited supplies are available (no firewood). For more information, phone Santee Lakes Regional Park.

SITES, FEES, FACILITIES, TIME LIMITS The campground has 152 numbered, full-hookup campsites. Each of the fees given in this paragraph is for one campsite per night. For lakefront sites with full hookups, the fee is $32 on Friday, Saturday, and holidays, and is $28 on other nights. For deluxe pull-through sites with full hookups, the fee is $28 on Friday, Saturday, and holidays, and is $26 on other nights. For regular full-hookup sites, the fee is $26 on Friday, Saturday, and holidays, and is $24 on other nights. For RV camping clubs, the fee is $22 on Friday, Saturday, and holidays, and is $19 on other nights; reservations are advised.

There are 55 primitive sites for tents or RVs (no hookups). The fee per site, per night, is $18 on Friday and Saturday, and is $20 on holidays (sites not available on other nights).

Each full-hookup site has a picnic table and a pedestal barbecue or a metal fire ring (with grill). The primitive, non-hookup area has about 30 picnic tables and a few barbecues. Camp roads are blacktop; sites are dirt and gravel. Parking spurs are blacktop or dirt and gravel. The maximum RV length is about 40 feet.

Phone for weekly and monthly camping rates. Reservations may be made up to six months in advance; phone for information.

The campground's restrooms have sinks, hot (pay) showers, and flush toilets. The camp has water spigots, drinking fountains, a coin laundry, propane, pay phones, soft drink and newspaper vending machines, trash cans, an RV dump station ($5 day-use fee), and RV storage areas (fee).

Picnic areas have picnic tables, pedestal barbecues, group shelters with large barbecues, and drinking fountains and restrooms nearby. The day-use fee per vehicle is $2 on weekdays and $3 on weekends or holidays. Reservations are advised for picnic groups.

Quiet hours at this camp are from 9 P.M. to 8 A.M. Dogs are not allowed in the day-use areas or at the pool, but are allowed in the campground. A dog-walking area is provided. The nightly fee is $1 per dog, and the limit is two dogs.

The campground at Santee Lakes is usually open all year. The camping limit is 30 days for RVs, and is 14 days for tents.

DIRECTIONS From I-8 in San Diego, take I-15 north 4.5 miles to State Highway 52 (freeway) in Tierrasanta. Take Highway 52 east about 7 miles to Mast Boulevard in Santee. Exit, turn left (east), and go 1.5 miles to Fanita Parkway. Turn right (south), and go a quarter mile to Carlton Oaks Boulevard. Turn right (west) and go a short way to the main entrance on the right.

Lake Jennings Regional Park

GENERAL SETTING (LOCATION, FEATURES, SUPPLIES, INFORMATION) Views of Lake Jennings to the east, or of Lakeside to the west, are afforded some of the campsites at this county park located east of Lakeside. Eucalyptus trees, pepper trees, and chaparral separate the sites and provide privacy and some shade. Cactus patches dot the campground. The park has about 100 acres.

This county park features hiking trails, a horseshoe pit, a playground, an enclosed pavilion that is reservable for groups, and an amphitheater (campfire center) with benches. Summer programs are sometimes given; phone for details.

Shore fishing is allowed daily, year-round, but boat fishing is allowed from Friday to Sunday only. The lake is stocked with trout in winter and catfish in summer. Fishing requires a day-use fee and a daily permit. A concession area (open weekends), a boat pier, and a boat launch ramp are located at the south side of the lake.

Lindo Lake County Park is a day-use park in downtown Lakeside that features a playground and a ball field.

Supplies and gasoline are available in Lakeside, about 2 miles west of the park, and in El Cajon, about 6 miles southwest. For more information, contact the San Diego County Parks' office.

SITES, FEES, FACILITIES, TIME LIMITS There are 35 family campsites with full hookups for RVs or pull-through trailers, for $16 per site, per night. There are 35 family campsites with electrical and water hookups for $15 per site, per night, of which 11 sites are for RVs or pull-through trailers, and 24 sites are for RVs or back-in trailers. Some sites are reservable, and the reservation fee is $3 per site. For each dog, the nightly fee is $1.

Non-hookup family campsites, for $12 per site, per night, include eight sites for pickup campers, vans, tent trailers, or tents; 12 sites for pickup campers or vans (not trailers); and 12 walk-in sites for tents.

All campsites are numbered. Camp roads are blacktop. Some parking spurs are blacktop, and other parking spurs are dirt and gravel, as are the campsites. The maximum RV length is about 35 feet at full-hookup sites, and about 25 feet at partial-hookup sites.

Most sites have a picnic table and have a pedestal barbecue or a concrete fire ring, or both. Some sites have wooden food lockers. The camp's restrooms have sinks and flush toilets; hot showers are available (not at all restrooms). The camp has water spigots, drinking fountains, a soft drink vending machine, pay phones, outdoor laundry tubs, outdoor sinks for fish cleaning, an RV dump station, and dumpsters.

The youth group area at the end of Bream Drive has lake views. The nightly fee is $35 for up to three nights. The area is reservable (no reservation fee) and accommodates 35 youths with required adult supervision. The youth area has picnic tables, a few pedestal barbecues, a concrete fire ring, and a small, partly enclosed pavilion with a few tables inside, a water spigot, a drinking fountain, trash cans, and a restroom nearby with a pay phone.

Lindo Lake County Park (day-use only) has picnic tables, barbecues, and restrooms; the day-use parking fee is $2 per vehicle.

No swimming is allowed in the lake. The campground is usually open the whole year. The camping limit is 14 days.

DIRECTIONS From I-15 in San Diego, take I-8 east about 16 miles to Lake Jennings Park Road in Lakeside (6 miles east of El Cajon). Go north about a mile. Follow the signs, turn right (east), and just ahead of the lake, turn left. Go about half a mile to camp.

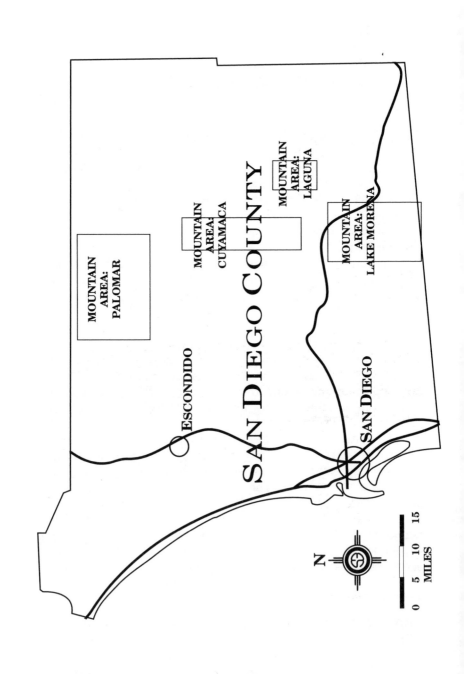

SAN DIEGO COUNTY

MOUNTAIN AREA: PALOMAR

MOUNTAIN AREA: CUYAMACA

MOUNTAIN AREA: LAGUNA

MOUNTAIN AREA: LAKE MORENA

ESCONDIDO

SAN DIEGO

N

0   5   10   15
MILES

SAN DIEGO COUNTY
MOUNTAIN AREA

Palomar Observatory, near Palomar Mountain State Park

SAN DIEGO COUNTY MOUNTAIN AREA

PALOMAR MOUNTAIN AREA

▲ 1. Crestline Group Camp
▲ 2. Observatory Campground
▲ 3. Fry Creek Campground
▲ 4. Palomar Mountain State Park
   Doane Valley Campground
   Cedar Grove Group Camp
▲ 5. Oak Grove Campground
▲ 6. Indian Flats Campground

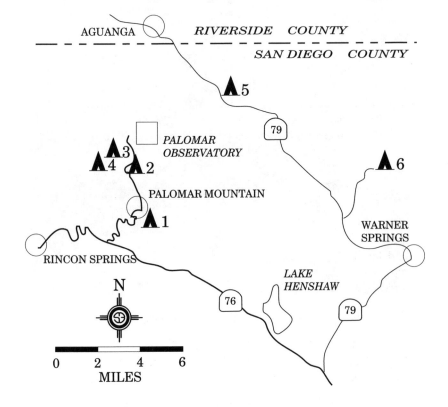

Crestline Group Camp

GENERAL SETTING (LOCATION, FEATURES, SUPPLIES, INFORMATION) This national forest tent camp for groups is located east of the small business crossroads of Palomar Mountain. It is set on the side of a low, pine-forested hill, just above the side road to camp which runs along the foot of the hill. The elevation is 4800 feet. Summer weather on Palomar Mountain is warm but cooler than in the local valleys. For more on Palomar Mountain and the Observatory, see Observatory Campground in this book.

Palomar Mountain County Park is not far east of camp, on a side road. It has a picnic area for day use only ($2 per vehicle), with restrooms; phone San Diego County Parks for details.

Supplies and gasoline are available in Julian, before making the trip to camp, and in Escondido, about 30 miles southwest of Highway S-7, via winding Highway S-6. Limited supplies, a pay phone, and a post office are available nearby, west of camp.

For further information, write or phone the Palomar Ranger District Office of the Cleveland National Forest.

SITES, FEES, FACILITIES, TIME LIMITS There is one group tent site, and the nightly fee is $75. The reservation fee for the site is $8.65. The group site accommodates 50 people and 12 vehicles (no RVs). The site has picnic tables, a fire ring with benches around it, water spigots, vault toilets, and a blacktop parking lot.

Crestline Group Camp is usually open from May 1 to November 30. The camping limit is 14 days.

DIRECTIONS From Julian, take State Highway 78 west about 7 miles to State Highway 79 in Santa Ysabel. Turn right (north) and go 7 miles to State Highway 76. Turn left (northwest) and go 4.5 miles to the Lake Henshaw area. At County Highway S-7, turn right (north) and go 11.5 miles. Follow the signs, and at the side road leading to camp, turn right (north) and go a short way to camp. (The side road to camp is just east of the intersection of County Highways S-7 and S-6.)

Observatory Campground

GENERAL SETTING (LOCATION, FEATURES, SUPPLIES, INFORMATION) World-famous Palomar Observatory is the source of this national forest campground's name. The camp is situated on a flat in the forested hills of Palomar Mountain, at an elevation of 4800 feet. Some campsites are shaded by pines and oaks, and other campsites are set out in the open. At times, a camp host resides in the campground.

Palomar Observatory is located about 2 miles north of camp, at an elevation of 5550 feet. Observatory Trail leads there, and the trailhead parking area is near the camp's amphitheater. Highway S-6 ends at the observatory's blacktop parking lot. Gus Weber Picnic Ground is set on a slight slope that drops away from the east side of this parking lot (no day-use fee). Picnic tables are set among boulders and shaded by cedars and oaks; no fires are permitted. High Point, the 6140-foot summit of Palomar Mountain, can be seen from the observatory area, and is about 2 miles east.

Supplies and gasoline are available in Julian, before making the trip to camp, and in Escondido, about 30 miles southwest of Highway S-7, via winding Highway S-6. Limited supplies, a pay phone, and Palomar Mountain's post office are available 2.4 miles south of camp, at the junction of Highways S-6 and S-7.

For more information, write or phone the Palomar Ranger District Office of the Cleveland National Forest.

SITES, FEES, FACILITIES, TIME LIMITS The campground has 42 nonreservable, numbered campsites for tents or RVs (no hookups), of which 13 sites accommodate trailers. The nightly fee is $12 per site. Some of the campsites are grouped in pairs and can be used as double sites for larger families (12 to 16 persons), for a nightly fee of $20 per double site. A vehicle parked for day use requires an Adventure Pass.

Some campsites have blacktop parking spurs, while others are walk-in sites in small groups that share small, blacktop parking areas away from the sites. The camp road is blacktop; sites are dirt and gravel. The maximum RV length is about 27 feet.

Each campsite has a picnic table and a pedestal barbecue or a metal fire ring (with grill), or both. The campground has water spigots, a drinking fountain, vault toilets, and dumpsters.

Observatory Campground is usually open from May 1 to November 30. The camping limit is 14 days.

DIRECTIONS Use directions for Crestline Group Camp, but stay on County Highway S-7, and shortly, at County Highway S-6, turn right (north). Go 2.4 miles, and at the campground's sign, turn right (east).

Fry Creek Campground

GENERAL SETTING (LOCATION, FEATURES, SUPPLIES, INFORMATION) Forests of fragrant cedars and pines, mixed with oaks, give plenty of shade to this national forest campground that sits in Fry Creek Canyon on Palomar Mountain. The camp is divided into two sections. One section lies just west of the entrance, with sites mainly on the canyon bottom. The other section is farther west, with sites higher up on the slopes of the canyon, where the narrow camp road is next to a drop-off on one side. The elevation is 4900 feet. For more on the area, see Observatory Camp.

For hikers, the 1.5-mile Fry Creek Trail circles Fry Creek Camp. If you drive in from the eastern part of the county, San Luis Rey Picnic Area is on Highway 76, about 6.5 miles west of State Highway 79, and about 2 miles west of Lake Henshaw.

Supplies and gasoline are available in Julian, before making the trip to camp, and in Escondido, about 30 miles southwest of Highway S-7, via winding Highway S-6. Limited supplies, a pay phone, and Palomar Mountain's post office are available 2.6 miles south of camp, at the junction of Highways S-6 and S-7.

For more information, write or phone the Palomar Ranger District Office of the Cleveland National Forest.

SITES, FEES, FACILITIES, TIME LIMITS The campground has 20 nonreservable, numbered campsites for tents or small RVs (no hookups). The nightly fee is $12 per site. Campsites are dirt and gravel. *Caution:* The road inside the campground is blacktop but is narrow. Parking spurs are blacktop, but are short and suitable only for small RVs; the maximum RV length is about 15 feet. A vehicle parked for day use requires an Adventure Pass.

Each campsite has a picnic table and has a pedestal barbecue, or a metal fire ring (with grill), or both. The camp has water spigots, vault toilets, and trash cans.

San Luis Rey Picnic Area has tables, fire grills, vault toilets, and a parking area. A parked vehicle requires an Adventure Pass.

Fry Creek Campground is usually open from May 1 to November 30. The camping limit is 14 days.

DIRECTIONS Use directions for Crestline Group Camp, but stay on County Highway S-7, and shortly, at County Highway S-6, turn right (north). Go 2.6 miles, and at the camp's sign, turn right (east). Again, this road is narrow.

Palomar Mountain State Park
Doane Valley Campground and
Cedar Grove Group Camp

GENERAL SETTING (LOCATION, FEATURES, SUPPLIES, INFORMATION) Views from many spots on Palomar Mountain extend to the ocean and are captivating. Summers are warm and fairly pleasant, and winters bring snow. Heavy annual rainfall results in rich cedar and pine forests and spring wildflowers. Palomar Observatory is only a few miles northeast of the state park, at the north end of Highway S-6 (see Observatory Campground). Nature walks and evening programs, given seasonally, focus on the mountain's plants, animals, and history. The park has nearly 1900 acres, and each camp's elevation is roughly 4000 feet.

Doane Valley Campground has family sites that sit within a small, funnel-shaped valley surrounded by somewhat steep slopes. Some sites sit on the valley floor, while others have been placed a short distance up the slopes. Cedars and oaks shade much of the camp and make a cozy atmosphere. Cedar Grove Group Camp, a developed camp for groups only, is set on slightly rolling terrain within a woodland of cedars.

The Doane Pond Day-Use Area, located near Doane Valley Camp, includes a picnic area in a mountain meadow surrounded by cedars and oaks. Doane Pond is stocked seasonally with trout by the Department of Fish and Game; trout fishing season is from November to June. Doane Valley Nature Trail connects the camp and the day-use area. Silver Crest Picnic Area is situated near the park entrance station.

Boucher Hill Firewatch Tower and another picnic area sit atop Boucher Hill at an elevation of 5400 feet, about a mile southwest of Cedar Grove Group Camp. The tower is closed, but you can hike up to it, have lunch in the picnic area, and enjoy the view. The state park's day-use parking fee is $2 per vehicle.

Supplies and gasoline are available in Julian, before making the trip to camp, and in Escondido, about 30 miles southwest of Highway S-7, via winding Highway S-6. Limited supplies, a pay phone, and a post office are available about 3 miles east of the state park, at the junction of Highways S-6 and S-7. From there, Palomar Observatory is 4.5 miles north, on Highway S-6.

Firewood is available at the state park entrance station. For more information, write or phone Palomar Mountain State Park.

SITES, FEES, FACILITIES, TIME LIMITS Doane Valley Camp has 31 numbered family campsites for tents or RVs (no hookups). The nightly fee is $12 per site. Reservations are advised from March 24 to November 30 (no reservation fee). The camp's road and parking spurs are blacktop; campsites are dirt. The maximum RV length is about 27 feet. Three sites are wheelchair accessible.

Each family site has a picnic table and a pedestal barbecue or a metal fire ring (with grill), or both. Some sites also have a wooden food locker. The camp has water spigots, an information board, and restrooms with sinks, hot (pay) showers, and flush toilets.

Cedar Grove Group Camp has three developed group areas, Areas 1, 2 and 3. The nightly fee for Area 1 is $32.50. The nightly fee for Area 2 or Area 3 is $20. Group reservations are recommended from March 23 to November 30 (no reservation fee).

At least nine persons are required in each of Cedar Grove's three camping areas. No more than 25 people are allowed at Area 1. No more than 15 people are allowed at either Area 2 or 3. Groups larger than these may reserve all three group camping areas. At least one supervising adult is required for each group of 15 youths who are 17 years old or under. Up to 10 vehicles are allowed at Area 1, and a pulling vehicle and trailer count as two vehicles. Parking spaces are rather small; the maximum RV length is about 21 feet. Areas 2 and 3 are tent camping areas that accommodate five non-camping vehicles each. The group camp's road is blacktop, and the grounds of the three group camping areas are dirt.

Each group area has picnic tables, fire rings, water spigots, and trash cans. Area 3 also has pedestal barbecues. Restrooms have sinks, hot (pay) showers, and flush toilets.

Picnicking facilities include tables, barbecues, restrooms, and parking lots. The day-use parking fee is $2 per vehicle.

Both campgrounds are usually open the entire year. The camping limit is 30 days at Doane Valley Campground, and seven days at Cedar Grove Group Camp.

DIRECTIONS Use directions for Crestline Group Camp, except at the junction of County Highways S-7 and S-6 continue straight ahead on S-7 for about 3 miles to the state park entrance station and ranger station. Continue about a quarter mile to the road to the camps (follow the signs), and turn right (north). Go 0.7 mile, and Cedar Grove Group Camp is on the left. Go 0.7 mile farther to Doane Pond Day-Use Area, then to Doane Valley Campground.

Oak Grove Campground

GENERAL SETTING (LOCATION, FEATURES, SUPPLIES, INFORMATION) This simply though pleasingly designed campground is located in and named after Oak Grove, a quiet little community with a few homes, located northwest of Warner Springs. This rural community's name describes the local scene—a fairly open valley dotted by clusters of oaks. Scattered ranches are among the few signs of civilization outside Oak Grove. The elevation at camp is 2800 feet. Local weather is pleasant much of the year for camping, but summers can be hot. Palomar Mountain is visible to the southwest.

Campsites are arranged in a cozy manner among three loops, and each loop is named for its predominant vegetation. Though the camp was named after Oak Grove, only the camp's Oak Loop features oaks as the predominant tree shading some of its sites. Ribbonwood Loop features ribbonwood trees with unusual swirled patterns on their dark bark, somewhat resembling the stripes on candy canes. On Chamise Loop, tall chamise bushes separate the campsites and provide privacy; trees shade some campsites.

The Butterfield Overland Stage Route passed through Oak Grove from 1858 to 1861, and the Oak Grove Stage Station building was built near the campground. Oak Grove Forest Station is across Highway 79 from camp, with a pay phone in front. The steep Oak Grove Trail can be reached behind the Forest Station, and it provides views of the valley.

The camp has an amphitheater (campfire center) with benches. At times, a camp host resides at campsite 29.

Oak Grove Community Hall, north of camp, can be rented for group events, and reservations are required. It has a stage, dance floor, tables and chairs, a kitchen, a nursery, and restrooms. Contact the camp host for information on this hall.

Supplies and gasoline are available in Temecula, near I-15. Limited supplies and gasoline are available on Highway 79 at Sunshine Summit, about 5 miles southeast of camp.

For additional information, write or phone the Palomar Ranger District Office of the Cleveland National Forest.

SITES, FEES, FACILITIES, TIME LIMITS The camp has 69 family campsites for tents or RVs (no hookups), and the fee is $15 per site, per night. There are 12 double sites for larger families

(12 to 16 persons), and the fee is $20 per double site, per night. The camp has nonreservable, numbered dirt sites. Camp roads and parking spurs are blacktop. The maximum RV length is about 27 feet. A vehicle parked for day use requires an Adventure Pass.

Each family campsite has a picnic table, and most sites have a pedestal barbecue or a metal fire ring (with grill), or both; a few sites have an old stone barbecue. Most double sites have two picnic tables and at least one pedestal barbecue and one fire ring. Restrooms at Oak and Chamise Loops have sinks and flush toilets; restrooms at Ribbonwood Loop have flush toilets (no sinks); some toilets are wheelchair accessible. The camp has water spigots, drinking fountains, dumpsters, and trash cans.

Oak Grove Campground is usually open throughout the year. The camping limit is 14 days.

DIRECTIONS From central Escondido, take I-15 north about 26 miles to State Highway 79 in Temecula. Exit and go east about 23 miles to the community of Oak Grove. The camp entrance is on the left (northeast) side of the highway.

Indian Flats Campground

GENERAL SETTING (LOCATION, FEATURES, SUPPLIES, INFORMATION) This national forest campground is tucked in the rugged backcountry hills north of Warner Springs and south of the San Luis Rey River. A rocky, boulder-covered hill stands adjacent to camp, forming an impressive backdrop. A huge boulder stands guard at the gate, a quarter mile from camp. Lost Valley Road leads to camp and follows a low ridge with views of the valley, and at some points, Palomar Mountain can be seen to the northwest.

Primitive campsites are situated along the camp's loop road. Oak trees shade much of the camp, manzanita bushes afford privacy, and cactus patches add contrast. The elevation is 3600 feet. Agreeable weather prevails most of the year. The weather, the water, and the oaks' acorns drew Native Americans to this area long ago. The Pacific Crest Trail crosses Highway 79 about half a mile south of Lost Valley Road. The camp has a small dirt parking area near the entrance.

Supplies and gasoline are available in Julian, by taking Highway 79 southeast about 23.5 miles from Lost Valley Road. Limited supplies, gasoline, and pay phones are available on Highway 79 in Warner Springs, about 2 miles southeast of Lost Valley Road, and at Sunshine Summit, about 7 miles northwest of Lost Valley Road.

For further information, write or phone the Palomar Ranger District Office of the Cleveland National Forest.

SITES, FEES, FACILITIES, TIME LIMITS The campground has 17 nonreservable, numbered campsites for tents or small RVs (no hookups). The nightly fee is $10 per site. The camp has a black-top loop road and dirt sites (no parking spurs). Parking is on the sites, which are small and suitable only for small RVs; the maximum RV length is about 15 feet. A vehicle parked for day use requires an Adventure Pass.

Each campsite has a picnic table and a metal fire ring (with grill); some sites also have a pedestal barbecue. The camp has drinking fountains, water spigots, vault toilets at two locations, trash receptacles, and information boards. Carry out your trash.

Caution: Lost Valley Road is blacktop, but is narrow and winding with some potholes. The side road to camp is dirt. Both roads are crossed by streams and are subject to flooding during rains.

Indian Flats Camp is subject to seasonal closure from March 1 to June 1 or July 31, for the protection of endangered species, but is usually open otherwise. The camping limit is 14 days.

DIRECTIONS From I-15 in Escondido, take State Highway 78 east about 35 miles to State Highway 79 in Santa Ysabel. Turn left (north), and go 16.5 miles (2 miles beyond Warner Springs) to Lost Valley Road (Forest Road 9S05). Turn right (northeast) and go about 6 miles to the gated, dirt side road that leads to camp. Turn left (west) and go about a quarter mile to camp.

SAN DIEGO COUNTY MOUNTAIN AREA

CUYAMACA MOUNTAINS AREA

▲ 1. William Heise Regional Park
■ 2. Cuyamaca Rancho State Park
▲ 2A. Los Caballos Horse Camp
▲ 2B. Los Vaqueros Equestrian Group Camp
▲ 2C. Paso Picacho Campground
▲ 2D. Green Valley Falls Campground

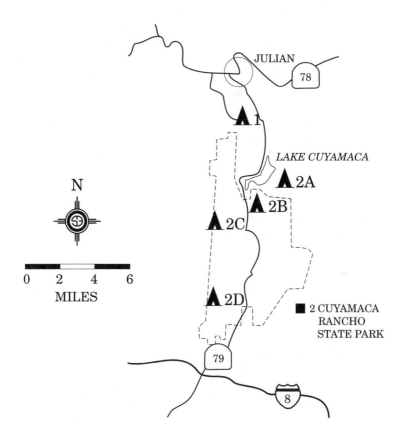

William Heise Regional Park

GENERAL SETTING (LOCATION, FEATURES, SUPPLIES, INFORMATION) Historic Julian is the focal point of the wooded valley of pines, oaks, and apple orchards in which this rural county park is located. Julian offers its visitors a village with western-style buildings that hint at its days as an old mining town, plus gift shops, the Julian Museum, tours of Eagle Mine, the Wildflower Show in May, and Julian Apple Days during autumn.

William Heise Park is set in a forest of oaks and has two picnic areas, a playground near the entrance, a horseshoe pit, and an amphitheater (campfire center) with benches and a rock fire ring. The park's size approaches 1000 acres; the elevation is more than 4000 feet. Desert View Trail provides desert and ocean vistas for hikers; it is steep and about 2 miles long. Kelly Ditch Trail leads equestrians south into Cuyamaca Rancho State Park and is over 5 miles long. The self-guided nature trail is a half-mile loop.

Santa Ysabel is a cute mini-version of Julian, and is located about 7 miles west of that town. Mission Santa Ysabel, an asistencia with a small museum, is about 1.5 miles north of Santa Ysabel. For information on Inaja Memorial Picnic Area, a mile southeast of Santa Ysabel, phone the Palomar Ranger District of the Cleveland National Forest. This picnic area is situated on a low hillside by the highway, and is partly shaded by pines. A plaque commemorates firefighters who perished in a local forest fire in 1956. A half-mile nature trail provides area views.

Supplies and gasoline are available in Julian, by taking Highway 78 east about a mile from Pine Hills Road. For more information, write or phone the San Diego County Parks' office.

SITES, FEES, FACILITIES, TIME LIMITS The camp has 40 family campsites for tents or RVs (no hookups), for $14 per site, per night, and 42 family campsites for tents only, for $12 per site, per night. Sites are reservable, and the reservation fee is $3 per site. Campsites are dirt and are numbered. Camp roads and parking spurs are blacktop. The maximum RV length is about 40 feet.

Each family site, for RVs or tents, has a picnic table and a metal fire ring (with grill) or a concrete fire ring (without grill). Each family site, for tents only, has a picnic table and a pedestal barbecue or a concrete fire ring, or both. The camp has water spigots, dumpsters, and restrooms with sinks and flush toilets (some with wheelchair access). Hot showers are available at restrooms in the tent area and near the RV dump station.

The group caravan area's nightly fee ranges from $125 to $150. This area accommodates 21 RVs and is reservable (no reservation fee). It has water spigots, a drinking fountain, picnic tables, a large brick barbecue, and a rock fire ring with four benches.

The park's RV dump station and a restroom with hot showers, sinks, and flush toilets are located near the caravan area. Outside this restroom are drinking fountains, newspaper and soft drink vending machines, a pay phone, and dumpsters.

Two youth group areas accommodate 30 youths each, with required adult supervision, for $35 per area, per night (up to three nights). Each areas is reservable (no reservation fee) and has picnic tables, pedestal barbecues, a rock fire ring, benches, water spigots, and an information board. One area is near the nature trail.

A few primitive cabins near Picnic Area 2 are available for $35 each, per night; phone for information.

The park's picnic areas have tables, pedestal barbecues, a few metal fire rings, restrooms, and parking lots. The day-use fee is $2 per vehicle. For each dog, the nightly fee or day-use fee is $1.

At Inaja Picnic Area in the Cleveland National Forest, a parked vehicle requires an Adventure Pass. Each of 10 picnic sites has a table and a pedestal barbecue. There are two vault toilets, information boards, and trash cans. Four blacktop picnic sites, the blacktop path and parking lot, and the toilets are wheelchair accessible.

The campground at William Heise Regional Park is usually open the whole year. The camping limit is 14 days.

DIRECTIONS From Julian, take State Highway 78 west about a mile to Pine Hills Road. Turn left (south), and go about 2 miles to Frisius Road. Turn left (east) and go about 2 miles to Heise Park Road. Turn right (south) and go a short distance to the park.

Cuyamaca Rancho State Park

Having nearly 30,000 acres, this is the fourth largest of California's state parks. Anza-Borrego Desert State Park, the largest, touches Cuyamaca State Park's eastern edge; other than this, these two state parks have little in common. Anza-Borrego presents a barren, dry, desert valley scene, whereas Cuyamaca is a forested, mountainous area with streams and an annual precipitation of more than 30 inches. *Cuyamaca* is of Kumeyaay Native American origin, and loosely translated means *rain above* or *rain beyond*. Summer weather in the Cuyamaca Mountains is fairly mild, and winter brings snow.

More than 100 miles of hiking trails reward the visitor with forest, meadow, and mountain vistas. Horseback riding is permitted on many trails. The luxuriant greenery of pine forests and oak woods contrasts beautifully with the bright colors of wildflowers during spring. Hawks, deer, raccoons, foxes, coyotes, bobcats, and mountain lions are among the park's residents. All features, including down wood and artifacts, are protected by law, and none may be removed.

The state park contains four developed campgrounds, one of which includes a group camping section, and two of which have facilities for equestrians. The elevation at each camp is roughly 4000 feet. Camp descriptions include other features of the area.

Cuyamaca Rancho State Park's headquarters, museum, and gift shop are housed in the historic stone ranch house, located near State Highway 79, about 9 miles north of I-8, in the sparsely populated Green Valley area. Julian and Pine Valley are supply points; for more about Julian, see William Heise County Park.

Cuyamaca Rancho State Park's free visitor guide has helpful information; to receive a copy, or for additional information, write or phone Cuyamaca Rancho State Park.

Los Caballos Equestrian Camp and Los Vaqueros Equestrian Group Camp

GENERAL SETTING (LOCATION, FEATURES, SUPPLIES, INFORMATION) The quiet country near Lake Cuyamaca is perfect for horseback riding, and these Cuyamaca state park camps are favorites of equestrians. One camp offers family sites, and the other offers group sites. Both camps feature horse corrals, troughs, and access to the California Riding and Hiking Trail. In Spanish, *Los Caballos* means *the horses*, and *Los Vaqueros* means *the cowboys,* and both are appropriate names for equestrian camps.

Los Caballos Equestrian Camp is set in a canyon flat, shaded by tall oaks and pines, and includes a day-use area with corrals, a few picnic tables, and water spigots. Los Vaqueros Equestrian Group Camp is set in a shady pine grove in a corner of a fairly open and oak-dotted valley. Lake Cuyamaca, located on the east side of Highway 79, about a mile north of the turnoff to the two camps, is not part of Cuyamaca Rancho State Park. The lake is stocked with trout, bass, catfish, and bluegill. Fishing requires a license, a permit, and a fee. Boats may be rented for lake use.

Night skies above Cuyamaca Rancho State Park are crystal clear at times. Star and planet watching parties are occasionally led by a ranger at a meadow near Stonewall Mine, near Los Vaqueros Camp; phone for details.

Supplies and gasoline are available in Julian, by taking Highway 79 north about 9.5 miles from the camps' access road. Limited supplies, gasoline, and a pay phone are available at Lake Cuyamaca's store. Paso Picacho Camp's store has limited supplies and is open limited hours. For more information, write or phone Cuyamaca Rancho State Park.

SITES, FEES, FACILITIES, TIME LIMITS Los Caballos Equestrian Camp has 16 developed equestrian family campsites (no hookups). The fee is $12 per site, per night, and includes two horses. Two extra horses are allowed per site, for $2 per horse, per night. Reservations are advised from April 1 to November 30 (no reservation fee). The day-use parking fee is $2 per vehicle. The camp has a dirt road and dirt sites (no spurs); parking is on the sites. The maximum RV length is about 27 feet.

Each family campsite has a picnic table, a metal fire ring (with grill), and two corrals. Some sites have wooden food lockers. The camp's restroom has sinks, hot (pay) showers, and flush toilets. The camp has water spigots, a pay phone, an information board, dumpsters, and recycling bins.

Los Vaqueros Equestrian Group Camp has one group campsite, and the fee is $150 per night. For reservations, at least nine persons and up to 80 persons are required. No more than 45 horses and 50 vehicles are allowed. Group reservations are advised from March 1 to November 30, and may be made no more than seven months ahead of time (no reservation fee). At least one adult's supervision is required for each group of 15 youths who are 17 years old or under.

The group site has picnic tables, fire rings, water spigots, dumpsters, and corrals. The restroom has sinks, hot (pay) showers, and flush toilets. The camp road and group parking lot are blacktop; the group site is dirt. The maximum RV length is about 27 feet.

Those who are camping with RVs at these two campgrounds may use the RV dump station at nearby Paso Picacho Campground.

Both equestrian camps are open most of the year, except during inclement weather. The camping limit is 30 days at Los Caballos Camp, and is seven days at Los Vaqueros Camp.

DIRECTIONS From I-15 in San Diego, take I-8 east about 32 miles. Exit at Japatul Road (State Highway 79). Go north about 13 miles to the access road with the sign that says HORSE CAMPS, STONEWALL MINE. Turn right (east), go a quarter mile, and Los Caballos Camp is on the right (south) side of the road.

Continue about half a mile farther (the road bends north), and at the side road leading to Los Vaqueros Camp, turn right (east). Go about a mile farther to the campground.

Paso Picacho Campground

GENERAL SETTING (LOCATION, FEATURES, SUPPLIES, INFORMATION) Stonewall Peak (elevation: 5730 feet) protrudes from the hills across the highway from this campground, located near the heart of Cuyamaca Rancho State Park. Campsites and day-use picnic sites are situated on gentle slopes rising from the floor of a small valley. Tall oaks and some pines shade much of the picnic and camping areas. Azalea Glen Trail passes between the main camp and group camp, and is named for its pretty flowers. Stonewall Creek Trail also passes through the area. Paso Picacho Nature Trail, an amphitheater (campfire center), and Paso Picacho Picnic Area are located near the entrance, and are accessed by the camp road that leads to the group camping section.

Lake Cuyamaca offers fishing, about 2 miles north (see Los Caballos Equestrian Camp). Visit Cuyamaca Rancho State Park's museum and gift shop, about 3 miles south. During summer, park staff or volunteers give Saturday night programs at the campfire center, and lead weekend nature walks that show visitors local plant life and wildlife. At times, a camp host resides in the family campground and sells firewood.

Supplies and gasoline are available in Julian, by taking Highway 79 north about 10.5 miles from the camps. Limited supplies and gasoline are available at Lake Cuyamaca's store. Paso Picacho Camp's store has limited supplies and is open limited hours. For more information, write or phone Cuyamaca Rancho State Park.

SITES, FEES, FACILITIES, TIME LIMITS The camp has 85 numbered family campsites for tents or RVs (no hookups). The fee is $12 per site, per night. Camp roads are blacktop and sites and spurs are dirt and gravel. The maximum RV length is about 27 feet. Some sites have blacktop spurs and are wheelchair accessible. Each site has a picnic table and a metal fire ring (with grill).

There are four undeveloped campsites at the back of the campground. You must park a quarter mile from these sites and walk to them. The fee is $7 per site, per night.

The group camping section has two group campsites, A and B, for tents. Due to limited parking space, no RVs are allowed, and no more than 20 non-camping vehicles per group site are allowed. The nightly fee for one group site (A or B) is $75. A group must have at least nine persons and up to 60 persons. For more than 60 persons (up to 120), both group sites may be reserved for $150 per night. At least one adult's supervision is required for each group of 15 youths who are 17 years old or younger. Group sites have tables, fire grills, a blacktop road, and dirt grounds.

Family and group camping sections have water spigots, hot (pay) showers, and restrooms with sinks and flush toilets (some with wheelchair access), and trash receptacles. The family section also has vault toilets. An RV dump station, a pay phone, and a newspaper vending machine are located near the entrance.

Reservations are available (no reservation fee). A few primitive cabins are available for $15 each, per night; phone for details.

Paso Picacho Picnic Area has picnic tables, pedestal barbecues, a water spigot, a restroom, a blacktop parking lot, and dirt grounds. Two wheelchair-accessible picnic tables are set on concrete slabs connected to concrete paths; they share a pedestal barbecue on the dirt. The day-use parking fee is $2 per vehicle.

Paso Picacho Campground is usually open all year. The camping limit is 30 days at family sites, and seven days at group sites.

DIRECTIONS From I-15 in San Diego, take I-8 east about 32 miles. Exit at Japatul Road (State Highway 79). Go north about 12 miles to the entrance, and turn left (west).

Green Valley Falls Campground

GENERAL SETTING (LOCATION, FEATURES, SUPPLIES, INFORMATION) Named for the local waterfall, this well-liked Cuyamaca State Park campground is located by Sweetwater River in Green Valley. In this area, the river is small enough that it tends to resemble a creek. The valley is indeed green, thanks to a forest of cedars, pines, and oaks in which this well-shaded camp and two picnic areas are situated. Some campsites are situated adjacent to boulders, some sites are set on an incline, and other sites are level.

Arroyo Seco Picnic Area is located at the north end of camp, and Falls Picnic Area is located at the south end of camp. Both picnic areas are tree-shaded. From Arroyo Seco Picnic Area, a hiking trail leads northwest about 1.5 miles to Arroyo Seco Camp, a hike-in camp, and about 5 miles farther to Cuyamaca Peak. Phone for information on Arroyo Seco Camp and another hike-in camp, Granite Springs Camp, on a hiking trail a few miles east of Green Valley Falls Campground. You must register at Cuyamaca Rancho State Park to camp at these hike-in camps.

Green Valley Falls is reached by a trail of less than a mile, and the trailhead is near Falls Picnic Area. Trailhead parking for Harvey Moore Trail is 0.7 mile north of camp, on Highway 79. Pine Ridge Trail leads southwest from the campground and offers terrific views of the Green Valley area.

The campground features a campfire center (amphitheater) with benches, located east of Arroyo Seco Picnic Area. Monument Trail leads northeast from the campfire center. Fishing is permitted in the creek-sized river during fishing season, when the river is stocked (license required). For fishing opportunities at Lake Cuyamaca, see Los Caballos Equestrian Camp.

The state park's museum and gift shop are located near Highway 79, about 2 miles north of camp. During summer, park staff or volunteers lead nature walks and give Saturday evening programs at the campfire center.

At times, camp hosts reside at sites 11 and 40 and sell firewood. Supplies and gasoline are available near I-8 in Pine Valley, about 12.5 miles southeast of camp, and in Julian, about 16 miles north of camp. Limited supplies are available about 5 miles north of camp at Paso Picacho Campground's store (open limited hours). For more information, contact Cuyamaca Rancho State Park.

SITES, FEES, FACILITIES, TIME LIMITS The campground has 81 numbered campsites for tents or RVs (no hookups). The nightly fee is $12 per site. Reservations are strongly recommended from March 27 to November 30 (no reservation fee). Camp roads and parking spurs are blacktop; sites are dirt. The maximum RV length is about 27 feet. Some campsites are blacktop and are wheelchair accessible.

Each campsite has a picnic table and a metal fire ring (with grill). The campground's restrooms have sinks, hot (pay) showers, and flush toilets (some with wheelchair access). The campground has water spigots, drinking fountains, an RV water and dump station, a pay phone, newspaper vending machines, information boards, and dumpsters.

Picnic sites at Falls Picnic Area and Arroyo Seco Picnic Area have picnic tables and pedestal or stone barbecues, or metal fire rings (with grills). Group picnic sites are also available. Some paths and picnic sites are blacktop and are wheelchair accessible, as are picnic area restrooms. Blacktop day-use parking lots for picnic areas and trailheads are provided. The day-use parking fee is $2 per vehicle.

Arroyo Seco and Granite Springs hike-in camps have a few campsites. Each camp has water seasonally and a pit toilet; no fires are permitted. The nightly fee is $1 per person.

Green Valley Falls Campground is usually open the entire year. The camping limit is 30 days.

DIRECTIONS From I-15 in San Diego, take I-8 east about 32 miles to Japatul Road (State Highway 79). Exit and turn left (north). Go about 7 miles to the campground entrance on the left (west) side of the highway.

Entrance to Paso Picacho Campground

SAN DIEGO COUNTY MOUNTAIN AREA

LAGUNA MOUNTAINS AREA

- ▲ 1. Laguna Campground
- ▲ 2. El Prado Group Camp
- ▲ 3. Horse Heaven Group Camp
- ▲ 4. Burnt Rancheria Campground
- ▲ 5. Wooded Hill Trailer Circle
- ▲ 6. Agua Dulce Campground

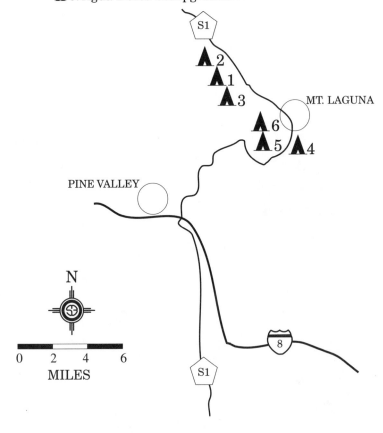

Laguna Campground

GENERAL SETTING (LOCATION, FEATURES, SUPPLIES, INFORMATION) The pine-covered Laguna Mountain Recreation Area is part of the Cleveland National Forest. Its six campgrounds include two developed family campgrounds, a primitive walk-in camp, a trailer circle, and two group camps, one with a wheelchair section. The recreation area offers a variety of trails, including nature trails, a hike-in camping trail in the Noble Canyon area, and the Pacific Crest Trail. It also offers two day-use picnic areas and the Mount Laguna Observatory. These attractions are discussed in the campground write-ups that follow.

The Laguna Mountain Visitor Center in Mount Laguna is staffed by volunteers and is open weekends and holidays. Sunrise Highway (County Highway S-1) is the lifeline of the area, and the tiny village of Mount Laguna is the area's only community. Kiosk-style map and information panels are provided on Sunrise Highway at the northern and southern ends of the recreation area.

Laguna Campground is the best equipped of the six camps in the Laguna Mountain Recreation Area. It is set in a fairly wide, shaded canyon that opens into Laguna Meadow to the west. At 5600 feet, winters are snowy and cold; summers are sunny, but not too warm; spring brings wildflowers. Oaks and fragrant pines shade many sites. For a pleasant hike, Big Laguna Trail leads west from camp through the meadow to Big Laguna Lake. The steep Lightning Ridge Trail is accessed near the amphitheater. It leads 1.3 miles up a hill with a view of the camp and the meadow.

The Pacific Crest Trail, located half a mile east of camp, on the eastern side of Sunrise Highway, can be accessed from a few points along the highway. The trail overlooks the Anza-Borrego Desert to the northeast and provides spectacular views.

The amphitheater (campfire center) has benches and a large fire ring; on summer Saturday evenings, campfire programs are given by staff volunteers. Summer programs about stars and planets are given at Mount Laguna Observatory; from camp, take Sunrise Highway south 4.5 miles to Norris Ranch Road, turn left (east) and go 0.25 mile to Star Party Trailhead parking area, partly blacktop; for information, contact the Laguna Mountain Visitor Center.

Pioneer Mail Picnic Area, 3 miles north of camp, has Pacific Crest Trail access, pine trees for shade, and a gravel trailhead parking lot for equestrians and other visitors. An information board describes the mail route from Texas to San Diego in the 1800s.

The Noble Canyon National Recreation Trail (5E04) and its upper (northern) trailhead are about a mile north of camp on the west side of Sunrise Highway. Across the highway on the east side there is trail access to the Pacific Crest Trail, next to the Penny Pines Monument honoring children who contributed pennies to the planting of trees in the national forest. Blacktop lanes for trailhead parking are provided on both sides of Sunrise Highway. The Noble Canyon National Recreation Trail offers 10 miles of hiking, horseback riding, and remote camping with no improved campsites or facilities. A parking area, water for horses, and vault toilets are provided down at Pine Creek Trailhead (the southern end of the trail) about 2 miles north of Pine Valley, off Pine Creek Road. No vehicles are allowed on the trail, between the two trailheads. A vehicle parked at the two trailheads requires an Adventure Pass.

At times, a camp host resides at campsite 96 and sells firewood. Supplies and gasoline are available in Pine Valley. Limited supplies (at Laguna Mountain Store and Lodge), a pay phone, newspapers, the Mount Laguna Post Office, and the Laguna Mountain Visitor Center (open limited days and hours) are available in the village of Mount Laguna, about 3 miles south of camp.

For more information, and for regulations on remote trail camping, including the required free Visitor Permit, write or phone the Descanso Ranger District Office of the Cleveland National Forest.

SITES, FEES, FACILITIES, TIME LIMITS The camp has 104 numbered campsites for tents or RVs (no hookups) of which 24 can accommodate trailers. The sites are divided among five loops and one stretch of road at the rear of camp, beyond the amphitheater. The loops are Meadow Loop, Shady Loop, Hillside Loop, Sunny Loop, and Roadside Loop. The nightly fee is $14 per site. Reservations may be made for sites at Meadow Loop and Shady Loop, and are $8.65 per site. Campsites are dirt, some with patches of grass. The camp's main road is blacktop; loop roads and parking spurs are dirt and gravel. The maximum RV length is about 40 feet.

Each campsite has a picnic table and a metal fire ring (with grill). The camp has water spigots, hot (pay) showers, flush toilets (some with wheelchair access), vault toilets, a pay phone at the entrance, and trash receptacles. An RV dump station is at Buckman Springs Rest Area, next to I-8, 4 miles east of Pine Valley.

Pioneer Mail Picnic Area has a few picnic tables and metal fire rings (with grills), vault toilets, a gravel parking lot, and a trash can (no water). A vehicle parked for day use at the picnic area or camp requires an Adventure Pass. Laguna Campground is usually open the entire year. The camping limit is 14 days.

DIRECTIONS From I-15 in San Diego, take I-8 east about 40 miles to Sunrise Highway (County Highway S-1) in Pine Valley. Exit and go north 12.5 miles. The camp is on the left (west) side of the highway; the sign says LAGUNA/EL PRADO CAMPGROUNDS.

El Prado Group Camp

GENERAL SETTING (LOCATION, FEATURES, SUPPLIES, INFORMATION) A specially designed, wheelchair-accessible section, Yerba Santa, is featured at this national forest group camp. The camp sits among pine groves near a meadow in the Laguna Mountain Recreation Area at an elevation of 5600 feet. In Spanish, *El Prado* means *the meadow*. Next door is Laguna Campground and nearby is the historic El Prado Cabin, an old ranger station. For more about the area, see Laguna Campground, which precedes.

Supplies and gasoline are available in Pine Valley. Limited supplies, a pay phone, the Mount Laguna Post Office, and the Laguna Mountain Visitor Center (open limited days and hours) are available in Mount Laguna, about 3 miles south of camp.

For additional information, write or phone the Descanso Ranger District Office of the Cleveland National Forest.

SITES, FEES, FACILITIES, TIME LIMITS Yerba Santa, the wheelchair-accessible section, is partly shaded by pines and has a view of the meadow. Its facilities include wheelchair-accessible picnic tables, pedestal barbecues, a fire ring, a water spigot, an information board, wheelchair-accessible flush toilets, concrete walkways with evenly spaced footlights, and trash cans. This group section accommodates 30 people, or it may be reserved as four family sites, with up to eight people per site. The nightly fee is $48 for the whole section, or $12 per family site within the section.

El Prado has four non-wheelchair group sections. Buckwheat accommodates 100 persons for $150 nightly. Big Sage accommodates 50 persons for $75 nightly. Manzanita and Whitethorn each accommodate 30 persons for $45 nightly, per section. Buckwheat accommodates 21 vehicles, and the three other sections accommodate seven vehicles each. These four group sections have picnic tables, barbecues, fire rings, water spigots, and vault toilets.

Reservations may be made and are $8.65 per group section. A sixth group camping section, Chokecherry, is for overflow camping only, and accommodates 20 people (phone for details and fee). Hot (pay) showers and a pay phone are available at Laguna Campground next door. An RV dump station is located at Buckman Springs Rest Area, next to I-8, about 4 miles east of Pine Valley. The group camp has blacktop camp roads.

El Prado Group Camp is usually open from the first weekend in May to Columbus Day in October. The camping limit is 14 days.

DIRECTIONS From I-15 in San Diego, take I-8 east about 40 miles to Sunrise Highway (County Highway S-1) in Pine Valley. Exit and go north 12.5 miles. The camp is on the left (west) side of the highway, and the sign says LAGUNA/EL PRADO CAMPGROUNDS.

Horse Heaven Group Camp

GENERAL SETTING (LOCATION, FEATURES, SUPPLIES, INFORMATION) This national forest camp in the Laguna Mountain Recreation Area is intended for groups of people, not horses, even though its name implies otherwise. It is located a short distance south of Laguna Campground, at a wide place in a pine-shaded canyon, near a meadow. Three group camping loops are set in open clearings surrounded by pines that separate the loops and give privacy. The elevation is 5600 feet. The Pacific Crest Trail is accessed at a few points along the east side of Sunrise Highway.

Supplies and gasoline are available in Pine Valley. Limited supplies (at Laguna Mountain Store and Lodge), a pay phone, the Mount Laguna Post Office, and the Laguna Mountain Visitor Center (open limited days and hours) are available in Mount Laguna, about 2.5 miles south of camp.

For more about this area, including observatory programs, see Laguna Campground. For more information, contact the Descanso Ranger District Office of the Cleveland National Forest.

SITES, FEES, FACILITIES, TIME LIMITS Lupine Loop accommodates 40 people and 10 vehicles for $60 nightly. Hollyhock Loop accommodates 70 people and 12 vehicles for $105 nightly. Buttercup Loop accommodates 100 people and 16 vehicles for $150 nightly. Reservations are $8.65 per loop. The group campsite at each loop is dirt. Campground and group loop roads are blacktop. The maximum RV length is about 27 feet.

Each group loop has picnic tables, metal fire rings (with or without grills), a water spigot, vault toilets, a dumpster, a blacktop parking lot, and dirt grounds. Hot (pay) showers are available at Laguna Campground. An RV dump station is provided at Buckman Springs Rest Area, next to I-8, 4 miles east of Pine Valley. Horse Heaven Group Camp is usually open from Memorial Day to Labor Day. The camping limit is 14 days.

DIRECTIONS From I-15 in San Diego, take I-8 east about 40 miles to Sunrise Highway (County Highway S-1) in Pine Valley. Exit and go north about 12 miles. The camp is on the left (west) side of the highway.

Burnt Rancheria Campground

GENERAL SETTING (LOCATION, FEATURES, SUPPLIES, INFORMATION) The little village of Mount Laguna, centrally located in the Laguna Mountain Recreation Area, lies north of this national forest campground. Cabins of the local village residents sit back among the pines and oaks, along the highway. The camp is set within a shady pine forest at an elevation of 6000 feet. At the place where the camp is situated, a rancheria was burned by the U.S. Cavalry in 1885. At times, a camp host resides in the campground.

Enjoy awe-inspiring views of the Anza-Borrego Desert and the distant Salton Sea from the Desert View Nature Trail and the Pacific Crest Trail. The Desert View Nature Trail begins in camp at the blacktop, day-use parking lot; this trail touches the Pacific Crest Trail in a few places. Desert View Picnic Area, located by Sunrise Highway, 0.7 mile north of camp, is partly shaded by oaks, and has views of the desert at some points. One picnic site is wheelchair accessible.

Summer programs are given at Mount Laguna Observatory. Take Sunrise Highway south 1 mile to Norris Ranch Road, turn left (east), and go 0.25 mile to Star Party Trailhead parking area.

Supplies and gasoline are available in Pine Valley. Limited supplies (at Laguna Mountain Store and Lodge), a pay phone, newspapers, the Mount Laguna Post Office, and the Laguna Mountain Visitor Center (open limited days and hours) are available in Mount Laguna, half a mile north of camp.

For additional information, write or phone the Descanso Ranger District Office of the Cleveland National Forest.

SITES, FEES, FACILITIES, TIME LIMITS The campground has 110 numbered campsites for tents or RVs (no hookups). The campsites are divided among six camping loops. The nightly fee is $13 per site. Reservations for campsites at Pinyon, Yucca, and Lilac loops are $8.65 per site. Campsites at Cherry, Redberry, and Mahogany loops are not reservable. The campground has blacktop roads and parking spurs and dirt campsites. The maximum RV length is about 27 feet.

Each campsite has a picnic table and a metal fire ring (with grill) or a concrete barbecue. Each camping loop has water spigots, flush or vault toilets, and a dumpster. Hot (pay) showers are available at Laguna Campground, 3 miles north. An RV dump station is located at Buckman Springs Rest Area, next to I-8, about 4 miles east of Pine Valley.

Desert View Picnic Area has picnic tables, metal fire rings (with grills), a drinking fountain, flush toilets that are wheelchair accessible, a dumpster, and a blacktop parking lot. A vehicle parked for day use at the picnic area or campground requires an Adventure Pass.

Burnt Rancheria Campground is usually open from May to September. The camping limit is 14 days.

DIRECTIONS From I-15 in San Diego, take I-8 east about 40 miles to Sunrise Highway (County Highway S-1) in Pine Valley. Exit and go north about 9 miles. Turn right (east) at the sign indicating the entrance to the camp.

Wooded Hill Trailer Circle

GENERAL SETTING (LOCATION, FEATURES, SUPPLIES, INFORMATION) This national forest camp is for groups with trailers and motorhomes (not tents). The camp is situated in the Laguna Mountain Recreation Area, on a slight slope on the side of a hill, at an elevation of 6000 feet. The air is pine-scented, and pines and oaks shade much of the trailer circle. The camp sign says WOODED HILL TRAILER CIRCLE; the camp is also referred to as Wooded Hill Trailer Loop.

Wooded Hill Nature Trail is a self-guided trail that wanders over difficult terrain. The trailhead is on the south side of the access road, opposite the entrance to camp, and has limited room for parking. Summer programs are given at Mount Laguna Observatory, across Sunrise Highway; take Norris Ranch Road east about a quarter mile to Star Party Trailhead parking area, partly blacktop; for details, contact the Laguna Mountain Visitor Center.

Supplies and gasoline are available in Pine Valley. Limited supplies (at Laguna Mountain Store and Lodge), a pay phone, a post office, and the Laguna Mountain Visitor Center (open limited days and hours) are available in Mount Laguna, about 1.5 miles north of camp. For more information, write or phone the Descanso Ranger District Office of the Cleveland National Forest.

SITES, FEES, FACILITIES, TIME LIMITS The trailer circle (group camping loop) accommodates 100 people, and the nightly fee is $165. The loop's reservation fee is $8.65. There are no hookups. The camp road and loop road are dirt. Dirt parking spurs surround a central area where most facilities are located. The maximum RV length is about 27 feet. For day use of the nature trail, an Adventure Pass is required for a parked vehicle.

In the center of the group camping loop are two long picnic tables, a large fire ring with two benches, water spigots, vault toilets, an information board, and a dumpster. Hot (pay) showers are available at Laguna Campground, about 4.5 miles north. An RV dump station is located at Buckman Springs Rest Area, next to I-8, about 4 miles east of Pine Valley.

Wooded Hill Trailer Circle is usually open from mid-May to mid-October. *Caution:* The dirt roads inside and outside the campground can become muddy and impassable during rainy weather. The camping limit is 14 days.

DIRECTIONS From I-15 in San Diego, take I-8 east about 40 miles to Sunrise Highway (County Highway S-1). Exit and go north about 8 miles to the access road to Wooded Hill and Agua Dulce Camps. Turn left (west) and go about half a mile to the camp entrance on the right (north) side of the road.

Agua Dulce Campground

GENERAL SETTING (LOCATION, FEATURES, SUPPLIES, INFORMATION) This primitive, walk-in tent camp is set among rustling, fragrant pines in a quiet part of the Laguna Mountain Recreation Area. The elevation is 5900 feet. This national forest camp is mainly for groups, but has a few individual tent sites.

Two group tent sites sit in a canyon bottom in the foothills near the eastern edge of a meadow. Individual tent sites are set on the lower slope of a hill, above the meadow. The dirt hiking trail to the campsites follows somewhat rolling terrain.

Summer programs are given at Mount Laguna Observatory, across Sunrise Highway; take Norris Ranch Road east about a quarter mile to Star Party Trailhead parking area, partly blacktop; for information, contact the Laguna Mountain Visitor Center.

Supplies and gasoline are available in Pine Valley. Limited supplies, a pay phone, the Mount Laguna Post Office, and the Laguna Mountain Visitor Center (open limited days and hours) are available in Mount Laguna, about 1.5 miles north of camp.

For further information, write or phone the Descanso Ranger District Office of the Cleveland National Forest.

SITES, FEES, FACILITIES, TIME LIMITS Wild Rose group site accommodates 50 people for $75 nightly, and is unshaded. The sign at the site says WILD ROSE, but the site is also referred to as Wildrose. Snowberry group site accommodates 25 people for $40 nightly, and is tree-shaded. Both group tent sites are reservable, and the reservation fee is $8.65 per group site. Each group site has picnic tables, metal fire rings (with grills), a large fire ring, a water spigot, vault toilets, and trash cans.

The four individual, walk-in tent sites are tree-shaded and nonreservable. The nightly fee is $10 per site. Most tent sites have a picnic table and a metal fire ring (with or without grill). The tent area has a water spigot, vault toilets, and trash cans.

A water spigot, a vault toilet, trash cans, an information board, and a dirt-and-gravel parking area are located near the camp entrance. Hot (pay) showers are available at Laguna Campground, about 4.5 miles north.

Agua Dulce Campground is usually open from Memorial Day weekend to Labor Day weekend. *Caution:* The dirt roads inside and outside the camp can become muddy and impassable during rainy weather. The camping limit is 14 days.

DIRECTIONS From I-15 in San Diego, take I-8 east 40 miles to Sunrise Highway (County Highway S-1). Go north about 8 miles to the access road to Wooded Hill and Agua Dulce Camps. Turn left (west) and go 0.7 mile. At the dirt entrance road to camp, turn right (north), and park in the parking area. Walk north on the dirt trail for about 600 feet to Wild Rose site, then walk about 300 feet to Snowberry site. Finally, walk about a quarter mile farther to the individual tent sites.

SAN DIEGO COUNTY MOUNTAIN AREA

LAKE MORENA AREA

▲ 1. Cibbets Flat Campground
■   Buckman Springs Rest Area
▲ 2. Boulder Oaks Campground
▲ 3. Corral Canyon Campground
▲ 4. Bobcat Meadow Campground
▲ 5. Lake Morena Regional Park
▲ 6. Potrero Regional Park

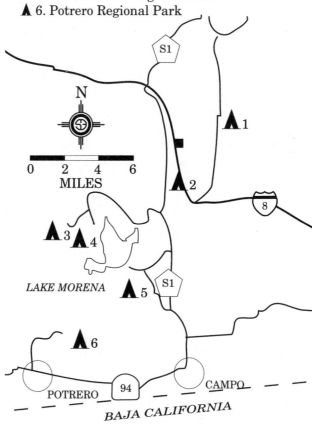

Cibbets Flat Campground

GENERAL SETTING (LOCATION, FEATURES, SUPPLIES, INFORMATION) This national forest camp, east of Pine Valley, is tucked in a secluded, oak-shaded glen on the lower eastern slope of the Laguna Mountains. Kitchen Creek Road affords views, along the way, of the valley to the east. Kitchen Creek flows through the area during winter. The elevation is 4200 feet. Summers are warm, and winters are cold, with snow at times on the mountains above. East of camp, Fred Canyon Road becomes a rough, restricted road, more like a trail; it reaches the Pacific Crest Trail, half a mile east.

Supplies and gasoline are available in Pine Valley. Limited supplies are available at La Posta Store on Old Highway 80, 1.5 miles east of Kitchen Creek Road. For more information, contact the Descanso Ranger District Office of the Cleveland National Forest.

SITES, FEES, FACILITIES, TIME LIMITS The campground has 24 nonreservable, numbered sites for tents or RVs (no hookups). The nightly fee is $10 per site. Campsites are dirt. The camp road and spurs are blacktop. The maximum RV length is about 27 feet. A vehicle parked for day use requires an Adventure Pass.

Each campsite has a picnic table and a metal fire ring (with grill). The campground has water spigots, drinking fountains, vault toilets, an information board, and trash cans. An RV dump station is available at Buckman Springs Rest Area, next to I-8, about 3 miles northwest of Kitchen Creek Road.

At times during summer, a camp host resides in camp. The campground is usually open all year. The camping limit is 14 days.

DIRECTIONS From I-15 in San Diego, take I-8 east about 46 miles (8 miles beyond Pine Valley) to Kitchen Creek Road (Forest Road 15S17). Exit, turn left (north), and go 4.5 miles to Fred Canyon Road (Forest Road 16S08). Turn right (east) and go to camp.

Buckman Springs Rest Area

This CALTRANS rest area in southeastern San Diego County has a good location between San Diego and the desert. Trees provide limited shade, and shelters provide shade at picnic tables. Some picnic tables are set on concrete slabs connected to the concrete pathways and are wheelchair accessible. Off the pathways, the grounds are dirt and gravel. The rest area's RV dump station serves several local campgrounds. The rest area has drinking fountains, water spigots, benches, pay phones, information boards, wheelchair-accessible restrooms, trash cans, and a pet area.

Supplies and gasoline are available in Pine Valley, 4 miles west. Pine Valley County Park has picnic tables, barbecues, a playground, a ball field, a restroom, pines, and oaks. Phone the San Diego County Parks' office for details; the park's day-use fee is $2 per vehicle.

To reach the rest area, from I-15 in San Diego, take I-8 east about 43 miles to Buckman Springs Road. Exit, turn left (east), go a short distance, and turn right (south) at the entrance. The rest area sits in a wide place between the freeway's opposing lanes.

Boulder Oaks Campground

GENERAL SETTING (LOCATION, FEATURES, SUPPLIES, INFORMATION) A tranquil, oak-spotted valley is the setting for this national forest campground, located about 6 miles southeast of Pine Valley. The valley is lush with sagebrush and manzanita. The surrounding hills are blanketed with chaparral and dotted with boulders. Boulders stand throughout the campground, and oak trees shade many campsites. The area and campground take their names from these features. The elevation is 3300 feet.

The valley includes Boulder Oaks and Buckman Springs, place names that represent a few ranches scattered throughout the area. Boulder Oaks used to have a store and a trailer park (both closed as of this writing). Buckman Springs has a developed rest area, and a school is roughly a mile west. About 2.5 miles east of Boulder Oaks is rural La Posta. The area is sparsely populated, compared to Lake Morena Village and Pine Valley, several miles away.

A special feature of this camp is the Horse Circle, an equestrian camping loop. Most equestrian sites have two corrals (most double sites have four). The Pacific Crest Trail passes by camp, and a dirt-and-gravel parking area is provided near the camp entrance. At times, a camp host resides in camp.

Supplies and gasoline are available in Pine Valley. Limited supplies are available at La Posta Store on Old Highway 80, about 2.5 miles east of camp. For more information, write or phone the Descanso Ranger District Office of the Cleveland National Forest.

SITES, FEES, FACILITIES, TIME LIMITS Of the 36 numbered campsites, 19 are nonreservable sites for tents or RVs (no hookups), for $10 per site, per night. There are 17 reservable equestrian sites with corrals for $12 per site, per night, and the reservation fee is $8.65 per site. Double sites are available. A regular double site is $20 per night, and an equestrian double site is $24 per night. The reservation fee is $8.65 per equestrian site, and is $17.30 per equestrian double site. The camp's roads, sites, and parking spurs are dirt. The maximum RV length is about 27 feet. A vehicle parked for day use requires an Adventure Pass.

Each site has a picnic table and a metal fire ring (with grill). There are water spigots, vault toilets (some with wheelchair access), and a dumpster. An RV dump station is at Buckman Springs Rest Area, 2 miles north, on Buckman Springs Road, next to I-8.

The camp is closed at times for the protection of endangered species; it is usually open otherwise. The camping limit is 14 days.

DIRECTIONS From I-15 in San Diego, take I-8 east about 43 miles. Exit at Buckman Springs Road (County Highway S-1) and go west to Old Highway 80. Turn left (south), and go about 2 miles to the camp entrance on the right (west) side of the road.

Corral Canyon Campground

GENERAL SETTING (LOCATION, FEATURES, SUPPLIES, INFORMATION) The Corral Canyon Off-Road Vehicle (ORV) Area, northwest of Lake Morena, was created by funds from California's Green Sticker program. Tall oaks shade this primitive national forest campground that sits in the bottom of Corral Canyon, at an elevation of 3500 feet. Some sites sit a little higher on the foot of an adjacent hill.

The ORV area has over 1200 acres. Each ORV trail has a sign that indicates what types of ORVs may be used and the trail's degree of difficulty. At Four Corners Trailhead, there is a gravel-and-dirt parking area and an ORV information sign. A four-wheel-drive trail (16S17) leads to the right (northwest), up to Los Pinos Mountain Lookout (4807 feet). About 2.25 miles east of the trailhead, via Corral Canyon Road, is an ORV trail. At the camp entrance, there is a small, dirt-and-gravel parking area for day use.

Per state regulations, "All vehicles must either be registered street-legal vehicles or have a State of California off-highway registration (Green Sticker)." ORVs are restricted to areas and trails designated for ORV use. ORV activity is not permitted in Lake Morena County Park, which has jurisdiction over the area between Four Corners Trailhead and Buckman Springs Road, and in that area, ORV activity is permitted only on Corral Canyon Road.

Supplies and gasoline are available in Pine Valley. Limited supplies and gasoline are available in Lake Morena Village. For

ORV regulations, ORV maps, and other information, contact the Descanso Ranger District Office of the Cleveland National Forest.

SITES, FEES, FACILITIES, TIME LIMITS The camp has 20 nonreservable campsites for tents or RVs (no hookups). Some campsites have parking spurs, and other sites share small parking areas. The camp road, campsites, parking spurs, and parking areas are dirt and gravel. The maximum RV length is about 27 feet.

An Adventure Pass is required for a street-legal vehicle parked at the campground or at an ORV trailhead. It is not required for an off-road vehicle with a Green Sticker.

Most campsites have a metal fire ring (with grill). The camp has two vault toilets and information boards, but has no tables or water. An RV dump station is provided at Buckman Springs Rest Area on Buckman Springs Road, next to I-8. Carry out your trash.

Corral Canyon Campground is usually open all year. The camping limit is 14 days. *Caution:* The roads closer to camp are one lane wide, with turnouts, and are blacktop with some potholes.

DIRECTIONS From I-15 in San Diego, take I-8 east about 43 miles. Exit at Buckman Springs Road (County Highway S-1) and go west. Just beyond Old Highway 80, stay on Buckman Springs Road as it turns south. Go about 3 miles and turn right (west) on Corral Canyon Road (Forest Road 17S04), which becomes a pot-holed blacktop road of one lane with turnouts. Go about 6 miles to the Four Corners Trailhead crossroads. Continue straight ahead (southwest) on Corral Canyon Road downhill for 1.5 miles to camp. The camp sign was missing, as of this writing.

Bobcat Meadow Campground

GENERAL SETTING (LOCATION, FEATURES, SUPPLIES, INFORMATION) This primitive national forest camp is located in the Corral Canyon Off-Road Vehicle (ORV) Area, at an elevation of 3800 feet. An ORV trail is provided. The camp is situated in a shallow, somewhat bowl-shaped depression on a low plateau. Oaks shade the campground, and boulders separate some sites. The side road close by camp runs along a low ridge, and has fine views of chaparral-covered Los Pinos Mountain (4807 feet) to the north, and of the surrounding rural valleys to the east, south, and west. Bobcat Meadows's bobcats keep hidden and are rarely seen.

Supplies and gasoline are available in Pine Valley and, though limited, in Lake Morena Village. For ORV regulations, see Corral

Canyon Campground in this book. For more ORV regulations, ORV maps, and other information, contact the Descanso Ranger District Office of the Cleveland National Forest.

SITES, FEES, FACILITIES, TIME LIMITS The camp has 20 nonreservable campsites for tents or RVs (no hookups). Some sites have parking spurs; other sites share small parking areas. Some portions of the camp road are blacktop; other portions are dirt and gravel. Sites, parking spurs, and parking areas are dirt and gravel. The maximum RV length is about 27 feet. Carry out your trash.

An Adventure Pass is required for a street-legal vehicle parked at the campground or at an ORV trailhead. It is not required for an off-road vehicle with a Green Sticker.

Most sites have a metal fire ring (with grill). The camp has two vault toilets, but has no tables or water. Buckman Springs Rest Area on Buckman Springs Road, by I-8, has an RV dump station.

Bobcat Meadow Camp is usually open all year. The camping limit is 14 days. *Caution:* The roads closer to camp are one lane wide, with turnouts, and are blacktop with some potholes.

DIRECTIONS Use directions for Corral Canyon Campground, but when you reach the Four Corners Trailhead crossroads, turn left (south), and go about a mile to Bobcat Meadow Campground.

Lake Morena Regional Park

GENERAL SETTING (LOCATION, FEATURES, SUPPLIES, INFORMATION) A peaceful country valley between Pine Valley and Campo is the setting of this 3000-acre county park set around a lake and meadow. Oaks, cottonwoods, poplars, and chaparral are plentiful in this area; wildflowers brighten the landscape during spring. Split-rail log fences add a rustic touch, as do the homes and cottages of Lake Morena Village. The elevation is 3000 feet.

The San Diego Railroad Museum, open weekends, is in Campo, about 6 miles south. The park has a boat rental area and a boat launch on the south shore. Use of your own boat requires a fee. *Caution:* Boulders are submerged in the lake. Fishing brings in trout and bass seasonally, and requires a daily permit and a fee. A fish-cleaning house with sinks is near the ranger station.

Enjoy the view to the north of the chaparral hills dotted with boulders. Boulders also dot the lake's shoreline. The main campground has developed sites for families and is set on the lake's south side, near the village. North Shore Campground, on the lake's north side, has primitive sites, some shaded by oaks and some separated by chaparral. The park's picnic area is near the centrally located ranger station. The enclosed pavilion (clubhouse) is in the main camp. The Pacific Crest Trail passes near the main camp. A few primitive cabins are available near the picnic area for $25 each, per night; phone for information.

Supplies and gasoline are available in Pine Valley. Limited supplies, gasoline, and a pay phone are available in Lake Morena Village, near the park's main campground. For more information, write or phone the San Diego County Parks' office.

SITES, FEES, FACILITIES, TIME LIMITS The family camping area at the main campground has 85 numbered family campsites. Of these, 57 sites have electrical and water hookups for RVs, for $16 per site, per night, and 28 non-hookup sites are for tents or RVs, for $12 per site, per night. Most sites are reservable, and the reservation fee is $3 per site. Campsites are dirt, with some grass. Camp roads are blacktop, and parking spurs are dirt and gravel. The maximum RV length is about 45 feet. Two blacktop campsites are wheelchair accessible. At times, a camp host resides at site 52.

Each family campsite has a picnic table and a concrete fire ring (without grill). The family camping area's restroom has sinks, hot showers, and flush toilets (some with wheelchair access). The family area has water spigots, an RV dump station, dumpsters, and trash cans. Drinking fountains and newspaper and soft drink vending machines are available outside the restroom.

The youth group area accommodates 35 youths, with required adult supervision, for $35 per night (up to three nights). It is reservable (no reservation fee), and has picnic tables, a group fire ring, water spigots, and a restroom nearby (no showers).

North Shore Campground, across the lake, has 11 primitive, numbered sites for tents or RVs in two sections. Oak Mesa section has sites 1–6, and Northridge section has sites 7–11. The nightly fee is $10 per site. Each site has a concrete fire ring (without grill). The camp has portable toilets, dumpsters, and an information board, but no water or tables. The camp has a dirt road and dirt sites, but no parking spurs; parking is on the sites. *Caution:* This road has some rough, rutty stretches and is muddy during rains.

The picnic area has picnic tables, pedestal barbecues, drinking fountains, water spigots, two vault toilets with wheelchair access, a dumpster, trash cans, and a blacktop parking lot. The day-use fee is $2 per vehicle.

For each dog, the nightly fee or day-use fee is $1. Lake Morena Regional Park's main campground and North Shore Campground are usually open all year. The camping limit is 14 days.

DIRECTIONS From I-15 in San Diego, take I-8 east 43 miles. Exit at Buckman Springs Road (County Highway S-1) and go west. Just beyond Old Highway 80, stay on Buckman Springs Road as it turns south. Go 3.5 miles to Corral Canyon Road (Forest Road 17S04). Turn right (west) and go 1.5 miles to North Shore Campground and turn left (south).

Continuing south on Buckman Springs Road, go about 2 more miles to Oak Drive, and turn right (west). Go 1.5 miles to Lake Morena Drive in Lake Morena Village. Turn right (north) and go half a mile to the park's main entrance.

Potrero Regional Park

GENERAL SETTING (LOCATION, FEATURES, SUPPLIES, INFORMATION) This inviting county park sits in a meadow near the little village of Potrero. Indeed, *potrero* is Spanish for *meadow* or *pasture ground*. Tall, large-limbed oaks shade the picnic area near the park's entrance. The shade is especially welcome during the hot summer in this mountain valley. The rest of the park is also somewhat shaded. The oaks' acorns provided food for Kumeyaay Native Americans who settled in this area before the 1800s.

The San Diego Railroad Museum is in Campo, about 10 miles east of the park, and is open on weekends; train rides are given. The park has a view of jagged, rocky Potrero Peak rising 2 miles west of the park. The peak's elevation is 3344 feet.

Near the picnic area are two playgrounds (one is farther away), two ball fields with benches (one also has bleachers), and an unenclosed dance pavilion with stage. An enclosed pavilion is at the caravan camping area. The park's self-guided nature trail passes a rock formation with holes made by the Kumeyaay people for grinding acorns. The park's elevation is 2300 feet.

Supplies and gasoline are available in El Cajon and Spring Valley; it is well to stock up before making the trip of roughly 30 miles to Potrero. Limited supplies and ice are available in Potrero, about 1.5 miles southwest of the park, on State Highway 94. For more information, contact the San Diego County Parks' office.

SITES, FEES, FACILITIES, TIME LIMITS There are 31 numbered, family RV campsites with electrical and water hookups.

The nightly fee is $12 per site. Camp roads, sites, and parking spurs are dirt and gravel; some roads are blacktop. The maximum RV length is about 45 feet. Site 32 is wheelchair accessible. Each family RV campsite has a picnic table and a pedestal barbecue or a concrete fire ring, or both. The family camping area's restroom has sinks, hot showers, flush toilets, and outdoor laundry tubs. The family area has water spigots, a drinking fountain (at the restroom), an RV dump station, and dumpsters.

There are seven developed, family tent sites, for $10 per site, per night. Each family tent site has a picnic table and a pedestal barbecue or a concrete fire ring. The tent area has water spigots and portable toilets. Most family RV sites and tent sites are reservable; the reservation fee is $3 per site.

The group caravan area accommodates 21 RVs in a circle around the pavilion. The fee for a group is $75 per night or $150 for the weekend, from 2 P.M. Friday to 2 P.M. Sunday. The caravan area is reservable (no reservation fee). It has picnic tables outside and inside the pavilion, pedestal barbecues, a large concrete fire ring, a water spigot, and trash cans. A restroom is nearby.

The youth group area, near the nature trail, accommodates 45 youths, with required adult supervision, for $35 per night (up to three nights). It is reservable (no reservation fee), and has picnic tables, two pedestal barbecues, a large concrete fire ring, a water spigot, a drinking fountain, portable toilets, and trash cans.

The picnic area has more than 25 tables, some pedestal barbecues, two serving tables under a shelter, a large brick barbecue, a water spigot, a drinking fountain, trash cans, a restroom nearby, a blacktop parking lot, and dirt grounds (some grass). Picnic groups (up to 300 people) require a reservation (fee). The day-use parking fee is $2 per vehicle. The nightly fee or day-use fee is $1 per dog.

A pay phone and a soft drink vending machine are provided outside the centrally located ranger station. Drinking fountains are available at restrooms.

The campground at Potrero Regional Park is usually open the entire year. The camping limit is 14 days.

DIRECTIONS From I-8 in San Diego, take I-5 south about 5 miles to State Highway 94 (freeway) and go east. After about 12 miles the freeway ends in Spring Valley, so stay on Highway 94 as it becomes a surface road, and continue for about 27 miles to Potrero Valley Road in Potrero. Turn left (north), and go 0.7 mile to Potrero Park Road. Turn right (east) and go a mile to the park.

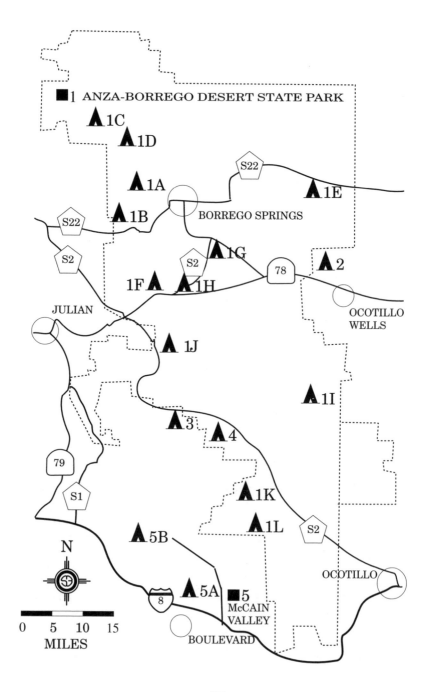

■1 ANZA-BORREGO DESERT STATE PARK

▲1C
▲1D
S22
▲1A
▲1E
S22 ▲1B
BORREGO SPRINGS
S2 ▲1G
1F▲ ▲1H
78 ▲2
JULIAN
OCOTILLO
WELLS
▲1J
▲1I
79
▲3
▲4
S1
▲1K
▲5B ▲1L
S2
N
OCOTILLO
▲5A ■5
8 McCAIN
VALLEY
0 5 10 15
BOULEVARD
MILES

SAN DIEGO COUNTY DESERT AREA

Borrego Valley with Santa Rosa Range in background

Anza-Borrego Desert State Park

At a whopping 652,000 acres, this is the largest state park in California. Set in the desert, with towering rocky mountains and rugged badlands, it is one of the nation's most geologically active areas. Fairly mild winters contrast with summers having temperatures of 110°. During spring, the barren landscape is decorated by wildflowers and cacti, including the large barrel cactus with its yellow flowers, and the beavertail cactus with its pink flowers; for details, phone the Wildflower Hotline. The state park offers a dozen, mostly primitive, campgrounds. Borrego Palm Canyon Campground and Tamarisk Grove Campground are the most developed and most easily accessible campgrounds. Borrego Palm Canyon Campground includes a group camping section. Campground descriptions include more about the desert's features.

The Visitor Center building, of trimmed natural stone, was cleverly built into the desert floor to fit in with the surroundings. The observation deck on the roof features information panels that identify local mountains and other points of interest, and the desert garden abounds with varieties of cacti and other desert plant life. The Visitor Center provides a complete stock of books and maps of the area. Rangers give lectures, and automated slide shows present the wildlife, plant life, and scenic geological features of the park. The Visitor Center is open daily, from October to May, and on weekends, from June to September. It is located at the end of Palm Canyon Drive, about 2 miles west of Borrego Springs, the region's town center and supply point.

The Visitor Center maintains a bulletin board on road conditions; check this board before driving on the desert's sandy dirt roads. These roads can become hazardous during sudden storms. Emergency call boxes are provided along Highway 78, in case of vehicle problems.

The Anza-Borrego Desert State Park Administrative Office (headquarters) is open weekdays, and is located on Palm Canyon Drive, a quarter mile east of the Visitor Center. The state park's free newspaper contains helpful information; phone the Administrative Office for a copy, or for additional information.

At campgrounds that have no barbecues or fire rings, an approved metal container off the ground may be used; phone for details. The day-use parking fee of $2 per vehicle is charged only at Borrego Palm Canyon Campground, Tamarisk Grove Campground, and Whitaker Horse Camp.

Borrego Palm Canyon Campground

GENERAL SETTING (LOCATION, FEATURES, SUPPLIES, INFORMATION) This is the largest and best equipped campground in Anza-Borrego Desert State Park. It is located in the Borrego Valley, 2.5 miles northwest of Borrego Springs, and about a mile north of the state park's Administrative Office (headquarters) and Visitor Center. A few palm trees add beauty to the campground, but little shade. The camp's elevation is 775 feet.

The Santa Rosa Mountains form the northern wall of the Borrego Valley. The bell-shaped Thimble Peak rises to the west in the rugged, rocky San Ysidro Mountains. Native Americans, attracted by mild winters, settled in this desert valley long ago.

The self-guided Borrego Palm Canyon Nature Trail reaches a palm oasis and a waterfall, 1.5 miles northwest of camp (3-mile round trip). The trailhead has a blacktop parking area and is at the west end of camp near the campfire center (amphitheater).

The steep Panoramic Overlook Trail, a round trip of 1 mile, offers hikers a view of Borrego Valley. The trailhead parking area for this trail and for the trail to the Visitor Center is near site 70.

Rangers, park staff, or volunteers conduct seasonal weekend campfire programs and nature walks that describe the wildlife and plant life, as well as the history and geology, of the local desert (see the park's free newspaper). A picnic area is provided.

At times, a camp host resides at site 21. Supplies, gasoline, a small outdoor mall, and art galleries are available nearby in Borrego Springs. The trailhead store at the west end of camp carries limited supplies (closed during summer). For more information, phone the Anza-Borrego Desert State Park Administrative Office.

SITES, FEES, FACILITIES, TIME LIMITS The family camping section has 117 numbered family sites, of which 52 are full-hookup sites for RVs (not tents), for $16 per site, per night, and 65 are non-hookup sites for RVs or tents, for $10 per site, per night. There are blacktop roads, blacktop or gravel spurs, and dirt sites. The maximum RV length is about 35 feet at hookup sites, and about 31 feet at non-hookup sites. Three wheelchair sites have blacktop spurs, dirt grounds, and picnic shelters.

Each family site has a picnic table and a metal fire ring (with grill) or a pedestal barbecue. A few sites have shelters. Water spigots, restrooms, and an RV water and dump station are provided.

The group section, for tents only, has five developed group sites. Each site accommodates 24 people. Together, the five group sites accommodate 120 people. The nightly fee of $18 per group site requires at least nine persons and a limit of six non-camping vehicles at each group site. At least one adult's supervision is required for each group of 15 youths who are 17 years old or under.

Each group site has some picnic tables, a large pedestal barbecue, a large shelter, a water spigot, and trash receptacles. A restroom with pay showers, a laundry tub, and a pay phone are nearby.

Restrooms in family and group sections have sinks and flush toilets (some with wheelchair access). Some restrooms have hot (pay) showers and outdoor laundry tubs. Drinking fountains, dumpsters, recycling bins, trash cans, and pay phones are provided.

All campsites are reservable, and reservations are recommended from October 1 to May 31. There is no reservation fee. If you are not reserving a site, bring water with you, in case all campsites are full, and it is necessary to find another camp in the area.

The picnic area has picnic tables, pedestal barbecues, picnic shelters, vault toilets, and parking. The day-use parking fee is $2 per vehicle at the picnic area or at the trailheads.

Borrego Palm Canyon Camp is usually open all year. The camping limit is 30 days at family sites, and seven days at group sites.

DIRECTIONS From Julian, take State Highway 78 east 18 miles to County Highway S-3. Turn left (north), and go 12 miles to Christmas Circle in Borrego Springs. From there, take Palm Canyon Drive west 1.5 miles to a crossroad with a sign that says 1 MILE TO CAMPGROUND. Turn right (north) and go a mile to camp.

Back at the crossroad, the state park's Administrative Office is on the south side of Palm Canyon Drive, and the Visitor Center is about a quarter mile west, at the end of Palm Canyon Drive.

Culp Valley Campground

GENERAL SETTING (LOCATION, FEATURES, SUPPLIES, INFORMATION) This very primitive state park camp is located in the hills between Borrego Springs and Ranchita, at an elevation of 3400 feet. Unimproved campsites are set in nooks and crannies where chaparral and boulders afford privacy. Logs serve as protective barriers. Creosote bushes and cholla cacti are among the kinds of plant life that live in the area. Interesting formations such as a pile of boulders can be seen at the eastern edge of camp. For hikers, Lookout Point Trail leads to Lookout Point, less than half a mile east of camp. It presents a terrific view of the Borrego

Valley to the east, and the rugged San Ysidro Mountains to the northwest, in which sits bell-shaped Thimble Peak, a natural landmark for early-era Native Americans. The Santa Rosa Mountains rise in the distance to the northeast. Pena Spring Trail leads to Pena Spring, less than half a mile northwest of camp.

For supplies and gasoline, take Highway S-22 east from camp about 9 miles to Borrego Springs. For more information, phone the Anza-Borrego Desert State Park Administrative Office.

SITES, FEES, FACILITIES, TIME LIMITS Several unimproved, unnumbered, nonreservable sites are available for tents or RVs. There is no fee. The camp's roads and sites are sand and dirt. The camp has no spurs; parking is on the somewhat small sites.

Two wheelchair-accessible vault toilets and information boards are provided, but no water or other facilities. Carry out your trash. The camp is usually open all year. The camping limit is 30 days.

DIRECTIONS From Julian, take State Highway 78 west 7 miles to State Highway 79. Turn north, and go about 11 miles to County Highway S-2. Turn right (east), go about 5 miles, and at the fork, bear left on County Highway S-22. Go about 9 miles to the camp's dirt entrance road at the camp's sign, and turn left (north).

Sheep Canyon Campground

GENERAL SETTING (LOCATION, FEATURES, SUPPLIES, INFORMATION) Remote Sheep Canyon, part of the mountainous Coyote Canyon backcountry, is the setting of this very primitive state park camp, located about 14 miles northwest of Borrego Springs. This is a backpacker's paradise for those who are experienced, and who understand the rigorous requirements of camping in mountainous backcountry areas. Stately palms stand out against the stark landscape. A stream flows seasonally, during fall and winter rains. The elevation is 1500 feet. Summer heat is intense.

Desert Gardens, located halfway between Borrego Springs and Sheep Canyon Camp, is a quiet place to stop, stretch, and enjoy the ocotillos. It was brought about by the Anza-Borrego Committee of the Desert Protective Council. This nonprofit group, dedicated to protecting the desert through donations, has set up an information board with panels describing local plant life and wildlife. Two picnic tables have been provided for day use.

Supplies and gasoline are available in Borrego Springs. For information, phone the Anza-Borrego Desert State Park Office.

SITES, FEES, FACILITIES, TIME LIMITS The camp has four primitive, nonreservable campsites for tents or four-wheel-drive pickup campers. There is no fee. The camp has no water or other facilities (chemical or pit toilets at times). Carry out your trash.

Note: Sheep Canyon Campground and the rugged dirt road that leads to it are usually open. Floods however have washed out a 1-mile stretch of dirt road near the campground. This stretch is closed to vehicles, at the time of this writing, so backpacking is currently the only way to reach the campground. Phone the Administrative Office for updates on road conditions before planning your trip to this remote area.

Caution: The area's rugged, rough dirt road, when open, is advised for four-wheel-drive vehicles, but not trailers or motorhomes. The camping limit at Sheep Canyon Camp is 30 days.

DIRECTIONS From Julian, take State Highway 78 east 18 miles to County Highway S-3. Turn left (north), and go 12 miles to Christmas Circle in Borrego Springs. Go east on Palm Canyon Drive a short way to DiGiorgio Road, and turn north. After about 5 miles, the pavement ends, and the dirt road is rough. Go a mile, and the road bends northwest. Go about 2 miles farther, and pass by Desert Gardens. Go about 3 more miles to the gate, and beyond that point, a very rough stretch of dirt road leads about 3 miles to camp.

Whitaker Horse Camp

GENERAL SETTING (LOCATION, FEATURES, SUPPLIES, INFORMATION) Vernon V. Whitaker, a state park volunteer for whom this equestrian camp was named, played an important part in its creation. The camp is located in a quiet area, perfect for horseback riding, in a wide cove in the desert foothills. Ocotillos and cholla cactus predominate, and mesquite trees afford limited shade. The camp features corrals, hitching posts, and a horse-washing area. The elevation is 960 feet.

An information board with rules for equestrians in the state park is located by the restroom. *Visitors must follow these rules, or this horse camp might be closed.* Overnight hobbling, tying to RVs, and makeshift corrals are prohibited.

Supplies and gasoline are available in Borrego Springs, about 7 miles south of camp, but horse feed is limited there, so you are advised to bring a sufficient quantity with you.

For additional information, phone the Anza-Borrego Desert State Park Administrative Office.

SITES, FEES, FACILITIES, TIME LIMITS The camp has 10 numbered equestrian campsites with two corrals at each site. The nightly fee, $10 per site, includes two horses and requires at least one horse per site. Two more horses are allowed per site for $2 per horse, per night. Reservations are advised from November to April (no reservation fee). The maximum RV length is about 24 feet.

Each site has a picnic table, a metal fire ring (with grill), and a pedestal barbecue. The camp has water spigots, a restroom with sinks and flush toilets, and recycling bins. Those who camp here with RVs may use Borrego Palm Canyon Camp's dump station. A shelter shades a few picnic tables next to a large pedestal barbecue, a large fire ring (without grill), and a sandy dirt parking area.

Whitaker Horse Camp is closed during some summers, but it is usually open otherwise. The camping limit is 30 days. *Caution:* The road to camp is powdery sand and dirt with washboard stretches, and can become impassable during inclement weather. This road is private, and visitors must drive slowly or it might be closed.

DIRECTIONS From Julian, take State Highway 78 east 18 miles to County Highway S-3. Turn left (north), and go 12 miles to Christmas Circle in Borrego Springs. Continue north on Borrego Springs Road about 3 miles to Henderson Canyon Road. Turn right (east) and go a short way to a sandy road with a sign that says HORSE CAMP. Turn left (north) and go 3.5 miles to camp. The sign at the campground says VERNON V. WHITAKER HORSE CAMP.

Arroyo Salado Campground

GENERAL SETTING (LOCATION, FEATURES, SUPPLIES, INFORMATION) This small, ultra-primitive state park camp is located nearly midway between Borrego Springs and the Salton Sea, the largest inland body of water in California. The sea is about 14 miles east of camp via the Borrego-Salton Seaway (County Highway S-22). Salton City, a small town, is passed about 2 miles before reaching the shore. The elevation at camp is 880 feet.

The camp sits on a little sandy flat surrounded by low rocky hills and mud hills. The sand affords a desert atmosphere, and ocotillos and creosote bushes are among the few signs of life. There is no shade. Four-foot-high log posts separate the sites.

Font's Point offers a striking view of the Borrego Badlands. Before taking the dirt road to the overlook, phone the Visitor Center for road conditions. From camp, take Highway S-22 west about 5.5 miles, turn left (south), and go about 4 miles to the overlook.

Supplies and gasoline are available in Borrego Springs, by taking Highway S-22 west about 19 miles from camp. For more information, phone the Anza-Borrego Desert State Park Office.

SITES, FEES, FACILITIES, TIME LIMITS The camp has a few small, unimproved, unnumbered sites for tents or small four-wheel-drive RVs. The camp's road and sites are powdery sand and dirt (also see below). There are no parking spurs; parking is on the sites. Several signs in camp show vehicle and camping rules.

There is no fee; sites are nonreservable. The camp has an information board and two vault toilets with wheelchair access, but no water or other facilities. Carry out your trash.

Arroyo Salado Campground is usually open throughout the year. The camping limit is 30 days. *Caution:* The very bumpy side road leading to camp is powdery sand and dirt, and is recommended for four-wheel-drive vehicles, but not trailers or motorhomes. Signs on the highway warn that this is a flash flood area.

DIRECTIONS From Julian, take State Highway 78 east 18 miles to County Highway S-3. Turn left (north), and go 12 miles to Christmas Circle in Borrego Springs. From Christmas Circle, go east on Palm Canyon Drive about 7 miles to Pegleg Road. Turn left (north), and go 3 miles to Borrego-Salton Seaway (County Highway S-22). Turn right (east) and go about 9 miles to a dirt side road leading to camp. Turn right (south), and go about a quarter mile to camp.

Yaqui Well and Yaqui Pass Campgrounds

GENERAL SETTING (LOCATION, FEATURES, SUPPLIES, INFORMATION) Named for local features, these two primitive camps are located about 2 miles apart and roughly 10 miles south of Borrego Springs. Having no facilities, Yaqui Pass Camp has the distinction of being the most primitive camp in Anza-Borrego Desert State Park, and it more nearly resembles a dirt parking area than a campground. The elevation is 1400 feet at Yaqui Well Camp, which sits near the foot of a grade in a narrow valley, and increases to 1730 feet at Yaqui Pass Camp, which sits at the pass on Yaqui Ridge.

Yaqui Well Campground's campsites are unimproved and separated by bow willows, mesquite trees, and small rocks. Yaqui Well, just west of camp, was a lifesaver for Native Americans, cowboys, and miners passing through the area, long ago. It is still a water source for birds pausing as they make their flight north. Ironwood trees provide them a home. An information board near the well describes the birds. Native Americans of an earlier era made arrowheads from the trees.

Yaqui Well Nature Trail is a short, self-guided tour. Tamarisk Grove Camp, across Highway S-3 from Yaqui Well Camp, has a ranger station and offers campfire programs and nature walks.

Yaqui Pass Camp's large, unpaved parking area for camping doubles as a day-use trailhead parking area for William Kenyon Overlook Trail. Surrounded on three sides by hills, Yaqui Pass Camp is open only to the highway.

William Kenyon Scenic Overlook commands a great view of the surrounding area, including the Pinyon Mountains to the south, and the Salton Sea to the east. The overlook is a quarter mile south of Yaqui Pass Camp, so this gives you a short but pleasant hike on William Kenyon Overlook Trail. Different kinds of cacti can be seen along the trail.

Supplies and gasoline are available in Borrego Springs, by taking Highway S-3 about 12 miles north from Yaqui Well Camp, and 10 miles north from Yaqui Pass Camp. For more information, phone the Anza-Borrego Desert State Park Administrative Office.

SITES, FEES, FACILITIES, TIME LIMITS Yaqui Well Campground has about 20 small, unimproved, unnumbered sites for tents or small RVs. The camp's roads and sites are sand and dirt. There are no parking spurs; parking is on the sites. Take care not to damage the vegetation. The campground has two wheelchair-accessible vault toilets, but no water or other facilities.

Yaqui Pass Campground is an open, primitive parking area for tents or RVs. The parking surface is dirt and sand, and is oiled periodically. The camp has no water, toilets, or other facilities.

There is no fee at either camp, and no reservations are taken. Carry out your trash.

Yaqui Well and Yaqui Pass Campgrounds are usually open all year. The camping limit is 30 days. *Caution:* The sandy dirt road in Yaqui Well Camp can become impassable during rainy weather.

DIRECTIONS From Julian, take State Highway 78 east about 18 miles to County Highway S-3. Turn left (north), go 500 feet, then turn left on a dirt road leading to Yaqui Well Camp. Continue north on State Highway S-3 about 2 miles to Yaqui Pass Camp on the right (east) side of the road.

Tamarisk Grove Campground

GENERAL SETTING (LOCATION, FEATURES, SUPPLIES, INFORMATION) Tamarisk (salt cedar) trees create a desert oasis at this campground, the second best equipped in Anza-Borrego Desert State Park. These greenish-gray trees somewhat resemble pines, and their shade brings relief from the intense summer heat. Local winter weather is pleasant for camping. The campground is located 12 miles south of Borrego Springs, at an elevation of 1400 feet. Many years ago, this was the site of a county prison camp.

Campfire programs are given at the amphitheater, and nature walks teach the visitor about the Anza-Borrego Desert and its diverse plants and animals. Rangers, park staff, or volunteers conduct these programs and walks. The state park's free newspaper has information. The picnic area is near the camp's entrance.

The mile-long Cactus Loop Trail, for cactus lovers, is across Highway S-3. Narrows Earth Trail, roughly 5 miles east of camp, via Highway 78, is a self-guided, nature trail loop of half a mile.

Supplies and gasoline are available in Borrego Springs; take Highway S-3 north 12 miles from camp. For more information, phone the Anza-Borrego Desert State Park Administrative Office.

SITES, FEES, FACILITIES, TIME LIMITS The camp has 27 numbered family sites for tents or RVs (no hookups). The nightly fee is $10 per site. Sites are reservable (no reservation fee). There are sand-and-dirt sites, blacktop roads, and rather short, blacktop parking spurs. The maximum RV length is about 21 feet. Site 27 is paved and is wheelchair accessible.

Each campsite has a picnic table, a picnic shelter with its campsite number on it, and a metal fire ring (with grill); the wheelchair site has a pedestal barbecue. The restroom has sinks, flush toilets, and solar (pay) showers. A portable chemical toilet with wheelchair access is also provided. The campground has dumpsters, recycling bins, and water spigots, but water is limited.

The picnic area has picnic tables and pedestal barbecues. The day-use parking fee is $2 per vehicle.

Those who camp at Tamarisk Grove with RVs may use the RV dump station at Borrego Palm Canyon Campground. Tamarisk Grove Camp is usually open all year. The camping limit is 30 days.

DIRECTIONS From Julian, take State Highway 78 east about 18 miles to County Highway S-3. Turn left (north), and the entrance is on the right (east) side of Highway S-3.

Fish Creek Campground

GENERAL SETTING (LOCATION, FEATURES, SUPPLIES, INFORMATION) This small, primitive state park camp is located in the Fish Creek-Split Mountain area, south of Ocotillo Wells. The elevation is 280 feet. Unimproved sites are separated by small rocks and dirt berms. The local desert landscape has a lonely, barren look. Ocotillos and creosote bushes are among the few signs of life at camp, along with desert willows in Fish Creek Wash.

Split Mountain and the Mud Hills, south of camp, are among the unusual natural formations. Split Mountain starts at the camp, and its dark brown, vertical stone walls create an awe-inspiring, cathedral-like skyline to the southwest.

Go hiking on Elephant Trees Discovery Trail, a self-guided nature trail, and see the rare specimens. Take Split Mountain Road north from camp about 2 miles. Opposite the Elephant Tree Ranger Station, turn (left) west at the dirt road. An information panel at this crossroad describes the trees. Drive to the end of the short dirt road, then hike the trail which is a loop of about a mile.

Hawk Canyon, about 5 miles west of Ocotillo Wells, and about 2.5 miles north of Highway 78, has three undeveloped walk-in sites. Phone the Administrative Office for information and for road conditions; the roads leading to the area are sandy and rough.

Only registered off-highway vehicles may be used at Ocotillo Wells SVRA, 9 miles north of camp, off Highway 78. A store in Ocotillo Wells (closed during summer) carries gasoline and some supplies. Supplies and gasoline are available in Borrego Springs at Highways S-22 and S-3, about 27.5 miles northeast of camp.

For additional information, phone the Anza-Borrego Desert State Park Administrative Office.

SITES, FEES, FACILITIES, TIME LIMITS Eight unimproved, unnumbered, nonreservable sites are available for tents or small, four-wheel-drive RVs. There is no fee. The camp has sand and dirt sites. There are no parking spurs; parking is on the sites.

Five sites each have a metal fire ring (with grill). The camp has an information board and two vault toilets with wheelchair access, but no water or other facilities. Carry out your trash.

Fish Creek Campground is usually open all year. The camping limit is 30 days. *Caution:* A stretch of road near camp is dirt and sand, some of which is powdery and deep, causing vehicles to lose traction or get stuck. Four-wheel-drive vehicles are strongly recommended, but not trailers or motorhomes. This road goes through Fish Creek Wash, subject at times to flash flooding. The Visitor Center in Borrego Springs maintains a bulletin on road conditions; contact the Visitor Center for updates. *Caution:* The camp's dirt entrance road is rocky, narrow, and inclined.

DIRECTIONS From Julian, take State Highway 78 east about 34 miles to Split Mountain Road in Ocotillo Wells. Turn right (south) and go about 8 miles. At the sign indicating the camp, turn right (west) onto a very sandy road. Go 1.5 miles to the camp's rocky entrance road and turn left (east).

Blair Valley (Little Pass) Campground

GENERAL SETTING (LOCATION, FEATURES, SUPPLIES, INFORMATION) This very primitive camp is located in Blair Valley, south of Little Pass. The elevation is 2500 feet. Southern Emigrant Trail caravans and Butterfield stage coaches passed through this valley in the 1800s. A sign near the camp entrance says that the Butterfield Overland Stage Route is half a mile east.

A dry lake bed divides the camp into two sections. No parking or camping is permitted in the dry lake bed; a sign says it is a closed area. The northern section is set at the foot of the hills and is an open camping area with little vegetation; a sign says to park adjacent to the roads on bare soil only. The southern section has unimproved sites separated by creosote bushes and partly shaded by mesquite trees. Agaves are seen on the highway near camp.

Native American pictographs (rock paintings) can be seen in Blair Valley. They are protected by law and may not be touched. Pick up a pictograph map at the Visitor Center in Borrego Springs, or at Tamarisk Grove. Desert author Marshal South once lived on Ghost Mountain, southwest of camp. A steep trail leads to the ruins of his home on the summit, and a view of the area.

Supplies and gasoline are available in Julian on Highway 78, about 16 miles northeast of camp, and in Borrego Springs at Highways S-3 and S-22, about 25 miles north of camp. Limited supplies and gasoline are available at Butterfield Ranch Store on Highway S-2, about 6 miles south of camp. For more information, phone the Anza-Borrego Desert State Park Administrative Office.

SITES, FEES, FACILITIES, TIME LIMITS The northern section is an open, primitive camping area. The southern section has several unimproved, unnumbered sites for tents or RVs. There is no fee; no reservations are taken. The camp's roads and sites are sand and dirt. There are no parking spurs; parking is on the sites.

The camp has an information board and two vault toilets with wheelchair access, but no water or other facilities.

The camp is usually open all year. *Caution:* The camp's roads are sandy dirt and can become muddy and impassable during storms. The camping limit is 30 days. Carry out your trash.

DIRECTIONS From Julian, take State Highway 78 east about 11 miles to County Highway S-2 (at Scissors Crossing). Turn right (south). Go about 6 miles to the sign that says BLAIR VALLEY at the sandy dirt road leading to camp, and turn left (east).

Mountain Palm Springs Campground

GENERAL SETTING (LOCATION, FEATURES, SUPPLIES, INFORMATION) Rocky, reddish-brown hills contrast beautifully with the desert's bright blue sky at this very primitive state park camp, and the desert quiet is appealing. The desert can be seen to the east through a window in the hills. The camp is located between Ocotillo and Agua Caliente Springs and has two sections. The western section is set back in a cove formed by low hills, and the eastern section is out in the open. Sites are outlined by little rocks. Some sites are separated by desert plants, including ocotillos, cholla cacti, and creosote bushes. The campground elevation is 760 feet.

Palm groves are scattered throughout the local area. From the camp's western section, two little palm groves can be seen to the north and northwest in canyons within the rocky hills. These groves are about a quarter mile from camp; trails lead to these groves and to other groves farther away.

The Carrizo Badlands Overlook, about 4.5 miles south of camp, on Highway S-2, provides a view eastward of the badlands in the foreground, and of the desert beyond, through a gap in the hills. The trail to the Well of Eight Echoes is accessed from County Highway S-2, about 1.5 miles north of camp.

Limited supplies and gasoline are available in Ocotillo on Highway S-2 near I-8, about 17 miles southeast of camp. Limited supplies are available at Agua Caliente Springs Store near Highway S-2, about 9 miles northwest of camp (open limited hours).

For additional information, phone Anza-Borrego Desert State Park's Administrative Office.

SITES, FEES, FACILITIES, TIME LIMITS Several unimproved, unnumbered, nonreservable sites are available for tents or RVs. There is no fee. The campground's roads and sites are sand and dirt. There are no parking spurs; parking is on the sites.

The camp has information boards (panels), and each of the two sections has a chemical toilet and trash cans, but no water.

Mountain Palm Springs Campground is usually open all year. The camping limit is 30 days. *Caution:* The roads to the campground and in the campground are sandy dirt and can become muddy and impassable during storms.

DIRECTIONS From Julian, take State Highway 78 east about 11 miles to County Highway S-2 (at Scissors Crossing). Turn right (south), and go about 28 miles. Turn left (west) at the dirt road that leads to camp, and go about a quarter mile to the entrance.

Bow Willow Campground

GENERAL SETTING (LOCATION, FEATURES, SUPPLIES, INFORMATION) This little camp is located in the desert hills northwest of Ocotillo. Local trees resemble willows but are actually desert catalpas, and Native Americans made bows and arrows from them. Smoke trees, mesquite trees, ocotillos (candlewoods), cholla cacti, and creosote bushes add interest to the desert landscape. The elevation at the campground is 950 feet.

This is the southernmost camp in Anza-Borrego Desert State Park. It is the least primitive of the state park's four camps south of Highway 78. The camp is situated in a crescent-shaped cove in the hills. Some sites are on flat ground; others are on a slight rise. A rocky, reddish-brown hill, north of camp, forms a backdrop.

The Carrizo Badlands Overlook, about 3.5 miles south of camp, on Highway S-2, provides views of the badlands and desert. Sombrero Peak (elevation: 4140 feet) is visible from the side road to camp. This rocky peak rises about 4 miles west of camp and is named for its resemblance to the familiar hat.

Morteros (grinding stones) and pottery fragments in the vicinity are the remains of an old Native American village. All artifacts are protected by law, and none may be removed, so that all visitors may enjoy them. Seasonal weekend evening campfire programs are given by park staff or volunteers. The state park's free newspaper has more information.

Limited supplies and gasoline are available in Ocotillo on Highway S-2 near I-8, about 16 miles southeast of the campground.

Limited supplies are available at Agua Caliente Springs Store near Highway S-2, about 10 miles northwest of the campground (open limited hours). For additional information, phone Anza-Borrego Desert State Park's Administrative Office.

SITES, FEES, FACILITIES, TIME LIMITS The campground has 16 nonreservable, numbered campsites for tents or RVs (no hookups). The fee is $7 per site, per night. The camp's roads and campsites are sand and dirt. There are no parking spurs; parking is on the sites. The maximum RV length is about 24 feet.

Each campsite has a picnic table, a metal fire ring (with grill), and a picnic shelter with its campsite number on it. *Caution:* The water spigot sign warns that the water must be boiled before using. The camp has two wheelchair-accessible vault toilets, information boards, trash cans, and recycling receptacles. The day-use parking area has a 30-minute limit.

Bow Willow Campground is usually open all year. The camping limit is 30 days. *Caution:* The side road leading to camp is dirt and sand, some of which is powdery, with washboard stretches. This road can become muddy and impassable during storms.

DIRECTIONS From Julian, take State Highway 78 east about 11 miles to County Highway S-2 (at Scissors Crossing). Turn right (south), and go about 29 miles. Turn right (west) on a sandy dirt road (which gets soft at times) and go 1.5 miles to camp.

Ocotillo Wells State Vehicular Recreation Area (SVRA)

GENERAL SETTING (LOCATION, FEATURES, SUPPLIES, INFORMATION) This state vehicular recreation area (SVRA) is located at the northern edge of the community of Ocotillo Wells. It lies within a wide desert valley surrounded by rocky, bare hills. North of the ranger station, the local landmark is flat-topped Borrego Mountain, rising to an elevation of 1200 feet. The SVRA is adjacent to the eastern boundary of Anza-Borrego Desert State Park, but it is a separate state park unit.

The SVRA has day-use recreation areas for the use of off-highway vehicles (OHVs). Only registered vehicles such as motorcycles, dune buggies, four-wheel-drive vehicles, all-terrain vehicles (ATVs), and other off-highway vehicles may be driven at the SVRA.

The SVRA has a number of open, primitive areas for camping or day-use parking, with few or no facilities. One of these areas is located east of the ranger station, on the east side of Ranger Station Road, near the large restroom.

The SVRA has three camping areas with family campsites and a few facilities—Main Street, the Quarry, and Holmes Camp. Main Street is located a mile east of the ranger station and is the closest camping area to Highway 78. The Quarry lies north of and between the ranger station and Main Street, and is spread out over a wide sandy area. Holmes Camp is located roughly 3 miles east of the ranger station, in a wide area partly shaded by mesquite trees.

The ranger station, located on the west side of Ranger Station Road, 2 miles west of the community of Ocotillo Wells, has a pay phone, information boards, and vault toilets.

Supplies and gasoline are available in Borrego Springs at Highways S-22 and S-3, about 16 miles northwest of camp. A store in Ocotillo Wells (closed during summer) carries limited supplies and gasoline. For information, phone Ocotillo Wells SVRA.

SITES, FEES, FACILITIES, TIME LIMITS Main Street has 18 sites, the Quarry has about 20 sites, and Holmes Camp has 28 sites. All sites are for tents or RVs. The only fee is the RV dump station fee, $2 per vehicle. The SVRA's roads and grounds are dirt, sand, and gravel. There are no parking spurs; parking is on the sites. There is no limit on RV size. The SVRA has no piped water.

Each site at Main Street, the Quarry, and Holmes Camp has a picnic table, a picnic shelter, and a metal fire ring (with grill) or a pedestal barbecue. Main Street and Holmes Camp have vault toilets (some with wheelchair access), trash cans, and dumpsters. The Quarry is a short way east of the large restroom.

The large restroom is located near the open area for camping and day-use parking on the east side of Ranger Station Road. It has sinks, vault toilets (some with wheelchair access), hot (pay) showers, and outdoor laundry tubs. Trash cans and dumpsters are provided. The RV dump station is on the west side of the road.

Ocotillo Wells SVRA's camping areas are usually open the whole year. The camping limit is 30 days. *Caution:* The SVRA's sandy dirt roads can become impassable during rainy weather. Roads in the Quarry are deep powdery sand, recommended for four-wheel-drive vehicles and suitable for dirt bikes.

DIRECTIONS From Julian, take State Highway 78 east about 31.5 miles to Ranger Station Road. Turn left (north) and go 0.25 mile to Quarry Trail. Turn right (east) and go 0.5 mile to the Quarry camping area. The SVRA's ranger station and an open camping

area are near the large restroom on Ranger Station Road. On Highway 78, continue east 1 mile to Main Street and its camping area
to the left (north). On Highway 78, continue east 2.25 miles to
Wolfe Well Road. Turn left (north) and go 0.5 mile to Holmes Camp
Road. Turn right (east) and go 0.25 mile to Holmes Camp.

Vallecito Regional Park

**GENERAL SETTING (LOCATION, FEATURES, SUPPLIES,
INFORMATION)** The location of this desert county park was the
site in the 1800s of the Vallecito Stage Station on the Butterfield
Overland Stage Route. The reconstructed building of brown adobe
brick stands today in the heart of the county park; information
panels have been placed on its front outside wall. The oasis was
once the site of a Kumeyaay village.

Vallecito means *little valley* in Spanish. The park does in fact
sit in a little desert valley surrounded by rocky, barren hills. Mesquite trees, a few palm trees, cactus gardens, creosote bushes, and
cholla cacti add to the park's desert atmosphere. The Laguna Mountains rise to the southwest, and are snowcapped during winter. To
the south, Red Top (a mountain) rises to an elevation of 4467 feet.
This 70-acre county park features a playground and a horseshoe
pit, and is adjacent to Anza-Borrego Desert State Park.

Supplies and gasoline are available in Julian on Highway 78,
before making the trip of about 29 miles to the park, or in Borrego
Springs at Highways S-22 and S-3, about 37 miles north of the
park. Limited supplies and gasoline are available at Butterfield
Ranch Store on Highway S-2, about 5.5 miles north of the park.
For more information, contact the San Diego County Parks' office.

SITES, FEES, FACILITIES, TIME LIMITS There are 44 nonreservable, numbered family sites for tents or RVs (no hookups). The
fee is $10 per site, per night. The park has a blacktop entrance
road and sand and dirt interior roads and sites (no parking spurs);
parking is on the sites. The maximum RV length is about 40 feet.

Each family site has a picnic table and a barbecue or a fire
ring, or both. Barbecues are pedestal or brick, and fire rings are
concrete or rock (without grills). Water spigots are provided.

The group caravan area is located at the park's north side. The
fee is $35 for one day and $70 for the weekend. The caravan area
is reservable (no reservation fee). It has picnic tables, two concrete fire rings, a rock fire ring, and a dumpster. A dirt-and-sand
parking lot is provided at the park's west side.

The youth camping area is at the park's south side. The fee is $35 per night, and adult supervision is required. The youth area is unshaded and has picnic tables, a large brick barbecue, and a rock fire ring. The youth area is reservable (no reservation fee).

The park's centrally located restroom has sinks and flush toilets (no showers). The park also has drinking fountains, dumpsters, and a pay phone near the entrance.

The picnic area has picnic tables, a large picnic shelter, pedestal barbecues, and brick barbecues. The day-use fee is $2 per vehicle. For each dog, the nightly fee or day-use fee is $1.

The campground is closed during summer, but is usually open the rest of the year. The camping limit is 14 days.

DIRECTIONS From Julian, take State Highway 78 east 11 miles to County Highway S-2. Turn right (south), and go about 18 miles to the park entrance on the right (south) side of the highway.

Agua Caliente Regional Park

GENERAL SETTING (LOCATION, FEATURES, SUPPLIES, INFORMATION) The Tierra Blanca Mountains provide a dramatic backdrop for this desert county park situated in a cove at the mouth of a canyon in Agua Caliente Springs. Palms, mesquite trees, ocotillos, and creosote bushes somewhat break up the park's white sand. Some sites sit next to the rocky foothills; some sites on a low rise have a view of the desert valley and the rugged Carrizo Badlands to the east. The park covers 910 acres, and is not part of Anza-Borrego Desert State Park, but is surrounded by it.

In Spanish, *agua caliente* means *hot water*. The park was named for local hot springs. It features a warm mineral water pool outdoors and a warm jacuzzi pool indoors. The ranger station, amphitheater, and picnic area are near the entrance. The park also has a playground, a shuffleboard court, a horseshoe pit, and a pavilion. Ocotillo Ridge Nature Trail is a short, half-mile loop that is not steep. Lengthier trails with steep portions include Moonlight Canyon Trail, Squaw Pond Trail, and Desert Overlook Trail.

Supplies and gasoline are available in Julian on Highway 78, before making the trip of about 33 miles to the park, or in Borrego Springs, at Highways S-22 and S-3, about 41 miles north of the park. Limited supplies and gasoline are available at Butterfield Ranch Store on Highway S-2, about 9.5 miles north of the park. Limited supplies are available at Agua Caliente Springs Store. For more information, contact the San Diego County Parks' office.

SITES, FEES, FACILITIES, TIME LIMITS There are 140 numbered family sites, 53 with full hookups for $16 per site, per night, and 53 with water and electrical hookups for $13 per site, per night. There are 34 developed, family tent sites without hookups for $10 per site, per night. Some sites are reservable; reservations are $3 per site. Camp roads and sites are sand and dirt and gravel; parking is on the sites. The maximum RV length is about 40 feet at full-hookup sites, and about 29 feet at partial-hookup sites.

Each family RV site has a picnic table and has a concrete fire ring (without grill). Most family tent sites have a picnic table and a pedestal barbecue. The family camp area has water spigots, drinking fountains, an RV dump station, and dumpsters. Restrooms have sinks, flush toilets (some with wheelchair access), and outdoor laundry tubs. Warm showers are located near the outdoor pool.

The group caravan area accommodates 10 to 20 RVs and has no hookups. The fee for a group is $75 per night, or $150 for the weekend which is from Friday at 2 P.M. to Sunday at 2 P.M. This area is reservable (no reservation fee), and has picnic tables, a fire ring, and water spigots. Restrooms and other facilities are nearby.

The picnic area has picnic tables, pedestal barbecues, and a parking area; restrooms are near the pools. The day-use parking fee is $2 per vehicle. A pay phone is located near the park entrance.

No pets are allowed. The camp is closed during summer, but is usually open otherwise. *Caution:* The sandy dirt roads can be impassable during rainy weather. The camping limit is 14 days.

DIRECTIONS From Julian, take State Highway 78 east about 11 miles to County Highway S-2. Turn right (south) and go about 22 miles. At Agua Caliente Hot Springs Road, bear to the right (southwest). Go 0.2 mile and pass the store, then go 0.4 mile to the park.

McCain Valley Resource Conservation Area
Lark Canyon and Cottonwood Recreation Sites

GENERAL SETTING (LOCATION, FEATURES, SUPPLIES, INFORMATION) Named for George McCain, a local homesteader and rancher during the mid-1800s, the McCain Valley is located north of the town of Boulevard and southwest of Anza-Borrego Desert State Park. The valley is broad, and many spots along McCain Valley Road have views. The In-Ko-Pah Mountains to the east are granite and have boulders and light chaparral. Balanced rocks (a rock sitting atop another rock) can be seen from McCain

Valley Road at several points. The McCain Valley is part of the transition zone that lies between the mountain and desert zones, and it features oak trees and manzanita bushes, as well as desert sagebrush.

The U.S. Bureau of Land Management has jurisdiction over the McCain Valley Resource Conservation Area and its two campgrounds, which have the names Lark Canyon Recreation Site and Cottonwood Recreation Site on their camp signs. The camps are somewhat primitive but inviting, especially Cottonwood, which is better shaded. The elevation at the two campgrounds is more than 3500 feet.

Lark Canyon Recreation Site's campsites are set on a slope on the foot of a hill. A few sites are shaded by oaks, but the rest of the camp is out in the open. The camp is divided into northern and southern sections, located about a quarter mile apart, and each section is divided into two subsections.

Cottonwood Recreation Site has campsites that are well shaded by oaks and are separated by sage and manzanita bushes. The camp sits on fairly flat ground on the valley floor. The camp's eastern and western sections are on either side of McCain Valley Road. The eastern section features corrals and hitching posts for horses. Pepperwood Trail, for horseback riding and hiking, leads from the camp's eastern section to Pepperwood Spring and to Sombrero Peak several miles northeast.

Off-highway vehicle (OHV) activity is permitted in the Lark Canyon OHV area. There are signs with OHV rules along McCain Valley Road and at Lark Canyon's camp. The OHV staging area is less than half a mile south of Lark Canyon's camp. Please observe all OHV rules, so that this activity may continue for everyone.

Carrizo Scenic Overlook and its picnic area are a quarter mile east of McCain Valley Road and about 3 miles north of Lark Canyon's camp. The overlook has a view of the Carrizo Corridor and the desert to the east, and of rocky Sombrero Peak which rises 4 miles north of the overlook. A diagram panel identifies the mountains in the area. There is a small, dirt-and-gravel parking area (no day-use fee) and a small, walk-in picnic area with two tables and a metal fire ring (with grill) among the boulders, sage, and cholla cacti. Lost Valley can be seen to the west.

Desert View Tower, roughly 12 miles east of Boulevard, and north of I-8, offers a view of the Imperial Valley. This small stone tower sits atop a circular building at an elevation of 3000 feet. A small museum and a gift shop are on the premises.

Supplies and gasoline are available in Pine Valley near I-8, roughly 20 miles west of the town of Boulevard. Limited supplies are available in the town of Boulevard, on Old Highway 80, about 2 miles west of McCain Valley Road. Gasoline is also available in Jacumba, next to I-8, about 8 miles west of McCain Valley Road. For ORV rules and for more information on McCain Valley and its two campgrounds, write or phone the El Centro Resource Area Office of the U.S. Bureau of Land Management.

SITES, FEES, FACILITIES, TIME LIMITS Lark Canyon Recreation Site has 30 unnumbered family campsites. Camp roads are dirt and gravel or sand. Parking is on the campsites or in dirt-and-gravel parking areas; there are no parking spurs.

Cottonwood Recreation Site has 25 numbered campsites. Camp roads are gravel; sites and parking spurs are dirt and/or gravel.

All sites at both camps are nonreservable and are for tents or RVs (no hookups). The nightly fee at each camp is $6 per site.

At both camps, each site has a picnic table, and most sites have a metal fire ring (with grill). Both campgrounds have vault toilets and trash cans. Water is available, but signs say it must be treated and purified before drinking; as a precaution, bring your own. An RV dump station is located at Buckman Springs Rest Area, next to I-8, about 16.5 miles west of McCain Valley Road.

Quiet time is from 9 P.M. to 8 A.M. throughout McCain Valley. Only down wood may be gathered for use as firewood in the two camps' fire rings. The maximum RV length is about 27 feet.

The camps are usually open all year. The camping limit is 14 days. *Caution:* McCain Valley Road is graded, but has some rough, washboard stretches; it and the campground roads can become muddy and impassable during storms. No off-highway vehicles may be driven on McCain Valley Road; they must be towed, transported by a trailer, etc., to off-highway areas.

DIRECTIONS From I-15 in San Diego, take I-8 east about 58 miles (roughly 20 miles east of Pine Valley), and exit at the town of Boulevard. Go right (south) about half a mile, to Old Highway 80. Turn left (east) and go about 2 miles. At McCain Valley Road, turn left (north); this road is blacktop for a short distance, then becomes a dirt road. Go 5.5 miles to Lark Canyon Recreation Site's southern section, and a quarter mile farther to the northern section. Continue north on McCain Valley Road, about 3 miles, and pass the turnoff to Carrizo Scenic Overlook (on the right). Go about 4 more miles to Cottonwood Recreation Site.

Appendix 1
San Diego Camping Directory

California State Parks
Reservations . . . . (800) 444-7275
California Department of Parks and Recreation . . . . (916) 653-6995
   Box 942896, Sacramento, CA 94296-0001
Anza-Borrego Desert State Park Administrative Office . (760) 767-5311
   Box 299, Borrego Springs, CA 92004
      Visitor Center . . . . (760) 767-4205
      Wildflower Hotline . . . . (760) 767-4684
Cuyamaca Rancho State Park . . . . (760) 765-0755
   12551 Highway 79, Descanso, CA 91916 . . . . (760) 579-1334
Ocotillo Wells State Vehicular Recreation Area . . . . (760) 767-5391
Palomar Mountain State Park . . . . (760) 742-3462
   Box 175, Palomar Mountain, CA 92060
San Elijo State Beach . . . . (760) 753-5091
   Mail to: 9609 Waples Street #200, San Diego, CA 92121
San Onofre State Beach—San Mateo Campground . . . . (949) 361-2531
      San Onofre Bluffs Campground . . . . (949) 492-4872
   Mail to: 3030 Avenida del Presidente, San Clemente, CA 92675
Silver Strand State Beach . . . . (619) 435-5184
   Mail to: 9609 Waples Street #200, San Diego, CA 92121
South Carlsbad State Beach . . . . (760) 438-3143
   Mail to: 9609 Waples Street #200, San Diego, CA 92121

San Diego County Parks
Reservations . . . . (858) 565-3600
County of San Diego Department of Parks and Recreation
   5201 Ruffin Road, San Diego, CA 92123-1699
      Office—Information . . . . (858) 694-3049

U.S. Bureau of Land Management (BLM)
El Centro Resource Area Office . . . . (760) 337-4400
1661 South 4th Street, El Centro, CA 92243-4561

U.S. Forest Service
Reservations . . . . (877) 444-6777
Cleveland National Forest Headquarters . . . . (858) 673-6180
   10845 Rancho Bernardo Road #200, San Diego, CA 92127-2107
Descanso Ranger District Office . . . . (619) 445-6235
   3348 Alpine Boulevard, Alpine, CA 91901
      Laguna Mountain Visitor Center, Mount Laguna (619) 473-8547
Palomar Ranger District Office . . . . (760) 788-0250
   1634 Black Canyon Road, Ramona, CA 92065-1205

Other Jurisdictions

Dixon Lake Recreation Area—Information . . . . (760) 839-4680
   Mail to: Public Works Department, 201 North Broadway,
   Escondido, CA 92025
      Reservations . . . . (760) 741-3328
Mission Trails Regional Park (City of San Diego) . . . . . . (619) 668-3275
   1 Father Junipero Serra Trail, San Diego, CA 92119
      Kumeyaay Campground—Ranger . . . . (619) 668-2746
      Lake Murray . . . . (619) 668-2050
Santee Lakes Regional Park . . . . (619) 596-3141
   Box 719003, Santee, CA 92072-9003 . . . . (619) 448-2482

Critter Safety

Big Bear Discovery Center, Big Bear Ranger District . . . (909) 866-3437
   Box 290, Fawnskin, CA 92333
California Department of Fish and Game . . . . (310) 590-5132
   330 Golden Shore, Suite 50, Long Beach, CA 90802
California Department of Health Services,
   Vector-Borne Disease Section . . . . (916) 324-3738
Cooperative Extension, UCSD . . . . (800) 200-2337
   UC Cooperative Extension–AHB,
   555 Overland Avenue, Building 4, San Diego, CA 92123
Los Padres National Forest . . . . (805) 683-6711
   6144 Calle Real, Goleta, CA 93117
Trabuco Ranger District, Cleveland National Forest . . . (909) 736-1811
   1147 East 6th Street, Corona, CA 91719-1616

Appendix 2
Rules and Regulations

Check-in time is 2 P.M., and *check-out time* is 12 noon at most campgrounds, including California State Parks and Cleveland National Forest campgrounds. At San Diego County Parks, check-out time is 2 P.M.

Six to eight persons is the usual limit per family (individual) campsite. The limit per double campsite is 12 to 16 persons. The limit per group campsite varies and is stated under each group campsite.

Youths under 18 years of age must be accompanied by a parent or guardian, or in San Diego County Parks, by a legally responsible adult.

Quiet time is observed from 10 P.M. until at least 6 A.M. at most campgrounds, but until 7 A.M. at most San Diego County Parks.

Generators must be turned off from 10 P.M. to 8 A.M. in California State Parks, and may not be operated in San Diego County Parks.

Fires are restricted to the barbecues, fire rings, fireplaces, fire pits, or other fire containers that have been installed at the campgrounds. An approved, portable metal container, off the ground, may be used at some campgrounds or camping areas that do not have fire containers; phone for details. No open ground fires are allowed. Fires are prohibited usually during fire season and periods of high fire danger.

Water is available at some camps, but where it is not, bring your own. *Caution:* Water from springs, creeks, and other natural sources is contaminated, so it must be treated and purified (by boiling, etc.), before drinking. During dry spells, water from natural sources is scarce.

Wood, flowers, plant life, wildlife, insects, rocks, artifacts, and other natural and man-made features are protected by law and may not be removed, collected, or gathered. Dead down wood may be gathered for use as firewood at McCain Valley's two campgrounds. Dead down wood may be gathered for use as firewood at some of the Cleveland National Forest campgrounds; phone the ranger districts for details. In camps where firewood may not be gathered (or is not sold), bring your own.

Trash and all other refuse must be placed in the receptacles provided. Where receptacles are not provided, please carry out your trash.

Vehicles must remain on established roads. Drivers must be licensed. Phone for regulations on motorbikes, trail bikes, and other vehicles.

Two vehicles is the usual limit per family (individual) campsite where vehicles are allowed. At many campgrounds, the fee per family campsite includes the vehicle that tows plus the vehicle that is towed. A second vehicle, driven in, may be allowed for an extra fee of $2 at national forest camps, county parks, Dixon Lake, and Santee Lakes, $3 at Kumeyaay Campground, and no extra fee at state parks or at McCain Valley. However, at some camps the vehicle being towed counts as the second vehicle for which the extra fee (or no extra fee) is charged. These rules are somewhat complex, so phone for details. The vehicle limit per group campsite varies and is stated under each group campsite where vehicles are allowed.

Recreational vehicles (RVs), including motorhomes, trailers, pickup campers, vans, van conversions, tent trailers, etc., must be self-contained where there are no hookups or sanitary dump stations available.

The maximum RV length has been given for some family (individual) and group camping sections, but may not apply at all campsites in a section. To determine if an RV length will accommodate a trailer, use the length from the trailer's hitch to the trailer's tail end. Many camps have RV lengths of 27 feet or less, and some camps can only accommodate RVs that are 15 to 20 feet long, such as pickup campers, van conversions, and small trailers. Some campgrounds that have some campsites for longer RVs include state beaches (30 to 35 feet), Borrego Palm Canyon (31 to 35 feet), Ocotillo Wells SVRA (no limit), county parks (35 to 45 feet), Santee Lakes (32 to 40 feet), and Kumeyaay (30 feet). If you have a long RV, reserve early at reservable sites, and arrive early at nonreservable sites.

Fishing at most campgrounds and day-use areas requires a valid California fishing license. A fee and/or a permit is required in some cases.

Hunting and firearms are not permitted in county parks, state parks, Dixon Lake Recreation Area, Mission Trails Regional park, or Santee Lakes Regional Park. Phone for regulations and restrictions on hunting and firearms in the Cleveland National Forest and in McCain Valley.

Dogs must be licensed, vaccinated for rabies, secured on a 6-foot leash, and confined at night in a tent or enclosed camping vehicle. Owners must clean up after their dogs. In state and county parks, dogs are not allowed at cabins, on trails, or near most water sources; phone for details. In national forests, dogs are not allowed near swimming areas. Regarding horses and other pets, phone for rules, regulations, and fees.

Closures of campgrounds, roads, and trails may occur due to fires, rains, floods, snows, slides, or other unforeseen emergencies. Otherwise, each campground is usually open during the periods stated in this book.

Wilderness and trail camping are beyond the scope of this book. Phone for special rules and regulations regarding these types of camping.

Rest areas and picnic areas may not be used for camping. Picnic areas are restricted to day use. At CALTRANS rest areas, no fees are charged.

Appendix 3
Adventure Passes

In places where camping or day-use fees are not charged in the Cleveland National Forest, an Adventure Pass must be displayed on the parked vehicle of anyone who visits this national forest for recreation. These places include campgrounds, picnic areas, trailheads, parking areas, OHV areas, and other places where vehicles are parked in the Cleveland National Forest. Recreation includes camping, picnicking, hiking, bicycling, horseback riding, swimming, skiing, fishing, hunting, and other activities.

A day pass costs $5. A year pass costs $30 (good until December 31). The fine is $100 for not displaying a pass. For clarification and more information, contact one of the Cleveland National Forest offices. The pass may be purchased at those offices and at many sporting goods stores.

Appendix 4
Desert Safety Rules and Tips

Vehicles should be well serviced before making any trips to the desert.

Hazards, such as roads in poor condition and inclement weather, must be known before planning a desert trip, so phone the local jurisdiction.

A *family member, friend*, or other reliable person should be informed which desert spot you will be visiting, and should watch for your return.

Items to take along in your vehicle include vehicle repair tools, a spare tire, flares, and a flashlight; many people usually have these in their vehicles. In your vehicle, also take extra water (at least a few gallons), nonperishable food, a first-aid kit, a tool kit, a shovel, a pocket knife, a compass, map(s), matches, a candle to light a fire (*obey all fire regulations*), a tarp for shade, a mirror for signaling, and a blanket (or large towel or rug, etc.) for daytime shade, nighttime warmth, and for signaling. Bring a hat, gloves, and clothing to protect you from the daytime sun and nighttime cold. Bring sunglasses and sunscreen for eye and skin protection.

Flash floods from unexpected storms are common in the desert. As a precaution, avoid washes, gullies, ravines, and other natural depressions.

Inoperative or stranded vehicles should not be abandoned. From a distance, a vehicle can be seen more easily by someone than you alone can be. The vehicle affords some shade during the hot daytime. If you must leave the vehicle, put a note on it stating which way you went and when, in order to aid search parties and law enforcement officials.

Signal to search parties by means of flares, or by flashing a mirror or other shiny object made of glass, metal, foil, or shiny plastic. Turn on the vehicle's emergency blinker lights, honk its horn, and put up its hood. Wave a blanket, towel, rug, tarp, or clothing (etc.).

For more rules and tips on desert safety, phone the jurisdiction of the desert campground you are interested in.

 # Appendix 5
Hazardous Critters

Usually the only creatures, other than humans, that may annoy campers are flies and mosquitos. While the probability of being struck by lightning is greater than being attacked by a mountain lion or bear, it is well to be aware that such creatures do exist in California's mountainous areas. The brochures listed below present information pertaining to these and other critters, and some precautions campers might take. The sources of these brochures are also listed below, and their phone numbers and/or addresses are given in the Directory (Appendix 1).

"Bear Us in Mind," Big Bear Discovery Center, Big Bear Ranger District, San Bernardino National Forest. (Pertaining to bears.)

"Bee Alert: Africanized Honey Bee Facts," Cooperative Extension, University of California, San Diego.

"Facts about Hantavirus in California," California Department of Health Services, Vector-Borne Disease Section. (Pertaining to deermice.)

"Facts about Lyme Disease in California," California Department of Health Services, Vector-Borne Disease Section. (Pertaining to ticks.)

"Facts about Plague in California," California Department of Health Services, Vector-Borne Disease Section. (Pertaining to rodents and fleas.)

"Living With California Bears," California Department of Fish and Game

"Living With Mountain Lions," California Department of Fish and Game. *Please report any close encounters with mountain lions, any attacks, and any sightings of dead or injured mountain lions to the California Department of Fish and Game.*

"Mountain Lion Territory," Trabuco Ranger District, Cleveland National Forest.

"Watch Out for These!" Los Padres National Forest. (Pertaining to rattlesnakes and poison oak.)

Index

*Group campsite(s) available.